NARRATIVE BIOGRAPHIES OF THE THOMPSON FAMILY GENEALOGY INCLUDING THOMPSON, HENSEL, GOODMAN, UPDEGROVE, PENMAN, BROWN (2), WORKMAN, CULP, RUSSELL, STODDART, GUISE, ROMBERGER, REISCH, SCHNECK, BLACK, MOFFATT, MUCKLE, LEHMAN, ANGST, SCHMIDT, COCHRAN, SMITH, KEITCHEN, WILSON, BOWMAN, WALTER, BRUCKER, PENNYPACKER, BENFIELD, HAMAN ET AL

MARC D. THOMPSON & TOM SULLIVAN

OTHER BOOKS BY AUTHOR

Compendium of Virtual and Traditional Fitness, © 2015, 978-0990807407

Fitness Book of Lists, © 2012, 978-0615656304

Fitness Quotes of Humorous Inspiration, © 2011, 978-0988344082

Genealogy of Anderson, Keefer, Gaugler, Livezly…, © 2014, 978-0988344037

Genealogy of Batdorf, Wert, Peters, Row..., © 2013, 978-0988344013

Genealogy of Duncan, Layman, McCloud, Overlander..., © 2014, 978-0988344020

Genealogy of Mazo, Curry, Thompson, Mason..., © 2010, 978-0988344075

Genealogy of Romano, Disimone, Vitale, Viviano..., © 2012, 978-0988344068

Genealogy of Thompson, Hensel, Goodman, Updegrove…, © 2013, 978-0988344044

Genealogy of Wittle, Acri, Stewart, Barbuscio..., © 2011, 978-098844051

Narrative Biographies of the Anderson Family Genealogy, © 2014, 978-500225681

Narrative Biographies of the Batdorf Family Genealogy, https://www.createspace.com/5064491 © 2014, 978-0990807414

Narrative Biographies of the Duncan Family Genealogy, © 2014, 978-1500123598

Narrative Biographies of the Romano Family Genealogy, © 2014, 978-1500405243

Poems...Of Eternal Moments, © 2012, 978-0-988344082

Thompson Family History, Vol X, Ed 5, © 2014, 978-1499352719

Virtual Personal Training Manual, © 2013, 978-0988344099

Family histories require constant revision. As this century moves along, more and more information becomes digitally or electronically disposable. If we do not save this information, it may be lost forever. Please contact author with any corrections or additions, marc@VirtuFit.net.

NARRATIVE BIOGRAPHIES OF THE THOMPSON FAMILY GENEALOGY INCLUDING THOMPSON, HENSEL, GOODMAN, UPDEGROVE, PENMAN, BROWN (2), WORKMAN, CULP, RUSSELL, STODDART, GUISE, ROMBERGER, REISCH, SCHNECK, BLACK, MOFFATT, MUCKLE, LEHMAN, ANGST, SCHMIDT, COCHRAN, SMITH, KEITCHEN, WILSON, BOWMAN, WALTER, BRUCKER, PENNYPACKER, BENFIELD, HAMAN ET AL

ISBN: 978-0990807421

MARC D. THOMPSON

Cover photograph Abel Thompson & Augusta Hensel, c 1905

www.VirtuFit.net - marc@VirtuFit.net

This volume is dedicated to all our family and friends, who selflessly donated information, time, effort, research and love to make this compilation possible.

ACKNOWLEDGMENTS

Thanks to my parents, to my sisters, to Ray from Pennsylvania State Library and to my hundreds of cousins who have donated their long-toiled family histories. Thanks to every clerk and registrar, cemetery manager, LDS employee, and ancestry.com staff, who have taken their time to assist in discovering our roots. This book is truly the love of thousands. Special thanks to Talea Jurrens, for her work in the first two narratives.

TABLE OF CONTENTS

FOREWORD

by Heather Thompson-Green

When I was asked to write the foreword for this book, I was honored, but not only because I feel it is an important part of this book, but because it is also my family history, and that makes me extremely proud to be a part of something so exciting. Marc D. Thompson is a dedicated author, with this Narrative being his 7th Volume including five generations. His interest in well-being is also evident to those who know him, and proven in his research. He is a self-motivated wellness coach who has a desire to pass along important family traditions and facts. He is inspirational to those who seek to understand their family line, and you will see that through his missional talent.

Family history, or genealogy, is not "just" history. It is where you came from, who you are, and what you pass on to those who follow. What we learn about ourselves can easily be traced back to where we came from, and understanding that is knowledge we take with us.

As you read this Narrative, it will inspire you to dig into your own genealogy and pass along interesting facts about the amazing family you come from. Perhaps, you will find a glimmer of a royal connection that will excite you, and lead you to investigate your history a little further. Tracing your father's, grandfather's, or great-grandfather's footsteps is not only educational, but fun.

Ancestry can be confusing to many, but it goes beyond just the word. It really connects you to a relative, and allows you to know their life, their travels, and their personalities. Seeing a picture that looks just like you might be enough for you to start enjoying your heritage, as Marc and I do.

Marc has done the hard part, so I hope you enjoy his work and dedication to our family lineage. Be the ambassador for your family as well, and enjoy the education of finding where your family began.

PREFACE

by Marc D. Thomspon

If I were given the opportunity to live in any era, I would most certainly pick the 1870s. The time was simple and the people were honest. Folks worked hard and took pride in their families, their homes and their reputations. When I look into the eyes of our ancestors from that time period, I feel a link; I would have fit nicely in their time.

Genealogy was created in order for people to know the history of their lineage, to discover their origins, and to prove blood-lines and royalty. This volume was compiled in response to our deep desire to understand and discover their past. It shall stand as part of the legacy of their ancestry. Our ancestors had remembrances. They had goals, glories, and personalities. The Irish kings would pass down their regal history orally. They would recite a list of names—their kin—noting outstanding events associated with the forebearers. The ancient Scottish bards similarly memorized their royal families, reciting the pedigrees of the Old Scot's Kings regardless of the complexity.

Our 35-year journey of knowledge has led to a plethora of information. We have learned much. We have discovered our roots—good, bad, and ugly. It has molded us. It has given us information on our health and ways to stay fit and healthy. It has given us photographs, the opportunity to see ourselves in generations gone by, noting how our features and personalities have evolved. It has helped with our jobs, our relationships, our lives. Our ancestors are a mirror of ourselves that can aide in our survival and understanding. Ancestry is wisdom.

We have discovered that we are related to some famous and infamous folks, and even found that there are some areas of the world named for our distant families. We are direct-line descendants of William Duke of Jülich-Cleves-Berg and Maria of Austria, Duchess of Jülich-Cleves-Berg, Countess Clothilde de Valois de Reni and Jacques de Sellaire, Von Zeller of Castle Zellerstein of Zurich, John Thomson of Haddington, Johann La Hentzelle of Lorraine, General John Benfield of Normandy, Henri Banage de Beauval of Rouen, Alexander Thompson of Schuylkill, the Guerne family of Eschert, the Bager family of Wiesbaden, the Emmerich family of Delkenheim, the Batdorf family of Darmstadt, the Gaukel family of Miltenberg and the Lotz family of the Palatinate.

We are direct-line descendants of soldiers who scaraficed for our freedom: Civil War servicemen Andrew G. Hensel and Daniel Updegrove, and possibly Elijah Anderson and Thomas E. Batdorf. War of 1812 servicemen Adam Frantz, Andrew W. Hensel and Joseph Workman, and possible William Row and John Gipe. Revolutionary War servicemen Andrew Messerschmidt, Andrew Miller, Frank Row, Henry Bucher, Jacob Lehman, Jacob Livezey, Jacob Philip Bordner, Jacob Rudy, John Adam Guise, John Balthaser Romberger, John Casper Hensel, John Conrad Bucher, John Daniel Angst, John Faber, John George Herrold, John George Schupp, John Henry Reiman, John Jacob Loyman John Miller, John Peter Braun (British), John Peter Shaffer, Jonas Rudy, Michael Garman, Michael Leyman, Nicholas Mantz, Peter Keefer, Valentine Welker, and William Anderson.

Our ancestors' names have been immortalized at these locations: the

Bager Homestead, Abbottstown, PA; the Chris Miller Homestead, North Lebanon Township, PA; the Benfield homestead, Berks Co., PA; the Livesey Homestead, Philadelphia, PA; the Wirth Homestead, Dauphin Co., PA; the Keefer Homestead in Berks, PA; the Morton Homestead in Chester, PA; the Herrold Homestead in Northumberland, PA; and the Jacob Lehman Homestead in Hanover, PA. Additionally, these place names were named after our forebearers: Bordnersville, Kelly Crossroads, Livesey Street, Herrold's Island, Keefer's Station, Deibler's Gap, Deibler's Dam, and Shoemakertown, all in Pennsylvania.

Our children's maternal lines include WWII servicemen Ed Mazo, Percy Forsythe and Robert Forsythe; WWI serviceman Raymond Barbush; and Civil War servicemen Cyrus Shannon, Jacob Wittle, John Shover, John Minnick, and Sebastian Shover. We are collateral descendants of Presidents Dwight D. Eisenhower and William McKinley; Pennsylvania politicians Samuel Pennypacker, John Morton, and Jonas Row; Civil War Brigadier General Galushia Pennypacker; entertainers Marlon Brando, Les Brown, and Ray W Brown; religious leaders Conrad Weiser and Michael Enderline; and famed Melba Dodge, Jesse Runkle, Enrico Caruso, and Galla Curci. Lastly, Taylor Wittel lists relations to James Madison, Zachary Taylor, Jefferson Davis, and Gene Autry.

At the moment, our paternal line breaks down to about 11/16 German, 2/16 Scottish, 1/16 French, 1/16 Swiss, 1/32 English, and 1/32 Dutch-Bohemian. Our maternal line breaks down to about 10/16 German, 4/16 English, 1/16 French, 1/32 Swiss and 1/32 Scandanavian. The approximate percentages of relativesirthplaces are: 45% born in Pennsylvania, 17% Germany, 14% Scotland, 9% Italy, 4% Georgia, 4%

South Carolina, 4% Ireland, 2% New York, and 1% Virginia, Florida, Switzerland, England, Bohemia, France, Sweden, Finland, and the West Indies.

Many genealogies tend to trace a descendant line or the paternal line (single ascendancy). Our purpose was to trace all ancestors with equal perseverance back in time. This is a monumental—if not near impossible—task. We have compiled a pedigree, beginning with our children and using an ahnentafel format. The emphasis at present is on generations 1 through 10, although we have completed research as far back as generation 21. Additional collateral ancestors have begun to be added as of 2015.

In most cases, the Anglicized first and middle names were used throughout the Narrative. For example, Johann Heinrich is John Henry and Orsala Francesca is Ursula Frances. The most commonly found surname was used, whether Anglicized or not. The majority of the collateral information was derived from the U.S. Census records and cousins' data.

Additionally, place names were documented as precisely as possible, using the name of the place as it was *at that time in history.* For example, parts of Germany were once Prussia, parts of Lebanon County, PA were once Lancaster County, PA. However in some cases, the common name was used. Before Pennsylvania's statehood, although it was the called the Province of Pennsylvania or the Pennsylvania Colony, simple Pennsylvania was used. This holds true to cities, provinces and countries as well. Lastly, to preserve privacy, all information on living persons has been removed or privatized.

The continued excellence of this genealogy will be improved through the following plan.

A. Correct errors and complete source citations.

B. Collect photographs and medical history of ancestors.

C. Document more biographical history of family.

D. Expound on current family group sheets and extend parentage.

E. Begin documenting the descendant lines.

We have a desire and we have a bond. We have a desire to know from whence we came. We want to know our history, our origins. We want to know what our ancestors did, how they persevered and how the spark of life made its way from Geoffrey Livesay, born 1410 in England, to Sophia, born 2004 in Florida. We feel that bond.

As this century moves along, more and more information becomes digitally or electronically disposable. If we do not save this information, it may be lost forever. The Thompson Family History is a guide for future generations who may use this information for their own goals, whatever they may be. We have given our children a foundation. Take it, improve it, embrace it. Read and enjoy.

BY THE NUMBERS

This volume will serve to honor us with the researched and documented information of our background. Our ancestry was derived from this data, the Thompson Family History (TFH) genealogy, which includes:

People:
3 Ancestors who died at sea: N. Benesch, G. Reith & G. Shoemaker
3 Ancestors named Ashley or Renae
8 Ancestors named Gerald or Gilbert
8 Most different ancestral lines with same surname: Miller, Mueller, etc
17 Number of children, one couple, Mary Louisa Peters/Thomas Edward Batdorf
22 Number of children, Isabelle Penman & Mary Bast/Alexander Thompson
24 Ancestors named Sophia or Marie
24 Most letters in name, male: Howard Andrew Carson Hensel
27 Most letters in name, female: Amelia Dorothy Elizabeth Bager
34 Ancestors named Andrew or Roman
50+ Most variations for single surname: Batdorf, Bodorff, Batterff, Pottorf, etc.
57 Ancestors named Connor or Adam
256 Ancestors named Shirley or Mary
569 Direct-line ancestors, Thompson lines
870 Direct-line ancestors
982 Total surnames, Thompson line
1,230 Total surnames
5,788 Relatives, Thompson lines
8,571 Relatives

Ages, Dates & Places:
5 Number of birth states
11 Number of birth countries
14 Youngest age having child, female: Anna Maria Hamm & Anna Barbara Knerr
17 Youngest age having child, male, John George Werner
18 Youngest age at death, female: Emma Keefer
30 Youngest age at death, male: William Duncan
50 Oldest age having child, female: Veronica Schmidt

59.6 Average lifespan, all lines
63.3 Average lifespan, Thompson lines
68 Oldest age having child, male: Alexander Thompson
94 Oldest age at death: Sarah Faber, Anna Bleymeyer & Michael Goodman
595 Place names, maternal lines
808 Place names, Thompson lines
1410 Earliest birth, unrecorded lines, Geoffrey Livesay
1689 Earliest birth, recorded lines, John Wendel George Traut

Miscellaneous numbers:
10 Generations, FTM lines only (numerous)
21 Generations, FTM & additional lines (Livesay)
34 Media records, collateral lines
79 Media records, maternal lines
254 Media records, Thompson lines
405 Sources used, maternal lines
830 Sources used, Thompson lines
5,750 Sources checked
26,266 KB TFH FTM File size

INTRODUCTION

by Marc D. Thompson

As Malcolm Gladwell says, "Who we are cannot be separated from where we're from." Genealogy is a duty. The day we were born or the day we bore children ourselves, we gained a responsibility of passing along our history. We are responsible for the knowledge of our parents and of our grandparents and all the wisdom that comes with this knowledge. Our duty, therefore, includes our children's heritage—including the names and faces of their forefathers and mothers, the medical history and genetic backgrounds of their blood lines, the princes and the paupers, the photographs and historical areas and properties, the tragedies and the joys.

These Thompson Family History (TFH) narratives are our heritage, and with this information we can be proud of ourselves and our past, and aim toward a bright future and better lives. If our duty is neglected, as each generation passes, so will our family history.

The mission of our genealogy books is to document and record all that is available of our ancestors and reap the enjoyment that these discoveries bring. The first goal is to amass photographs—as a face can tell a thousand tales—as so much can be learned from them. The second goal of our research is to document the medical background of our ancestors, so our children can lead a healthier life.

The third goal is to continue to extend the lineage in order to link to as many relatives as possible. Our ancestors are not mere names or dates—they have tales to tell, journeys to document, lives to discover. They have accomplishments and setbacks, which in turn help us with ours. Our final goal leads us to the building of narratives from this amassed information, producing a readable experience of our ancestors and their lives. This is one of several narrative genealogies produced from the amazing amount of documented data. As we mentioned "Who we are cannot be separated from where we're from," this book therefore allows us to know precisely where we're from.

CHAPTER 1

ABEL ROBERT THOMPSON
&
GUSSIE MAE HENSEL

ABEL ROBERT THOMPSON & GUSSIE MAE HENSEL

Abel Robert Thompson came into this world on the eve of another cold Pennsylvania winter. He was born on November 28, 1880, to proud parents, Robert Bruce Thompson and Lydia Ann Goodman both Pennsylvania natives living in Sheridan at the time. Carrying on the family tradition of honoring their ancestors, Abel bore the middle name Robert, his father's name. Abel's family had a long and important history in the area where he was born and grew up. The town of Sheridan was laid by his grandfather, Alexander Thompson, on his former lands. Grandfather Alexander was the first to sell coal from the area, later known as the York Farm Colliery, and Alexander was the owner of Thompson's Mill.

Just two days after the celebration of St. Valentine's Day, February 16, 1885, an adorable baby girl was born to Howard Andrew Carson Hensel and Clara Matilda Updegrove. She was baptized Augusta Mae on April 5, 1885, in Dauphin County, Pennsylvania. Gussie, as she was fondly known, grew up during the staunch age of Victorianism. She was able to attend school only until the fifth grade. Being the oldest of eleven children, her formal education was cut short when it became necessary for Gussie to begin assisting in the household duties and the care of her siblings. With so many mouths to feed in the family, it was later necessary for her to become an additional bread winner—as a teen, she was employed as a domestic servant. However, it wouldn't be long before she would move on to married life.

When Gussie met Abel, he was working as a general laborer. He was a tall, handsome man with dark hair, grey eyes, and a lean physique from the efforts of his occupation. Gussie never had eyes for any other man. She was a lovely June bride dressed in flowing white when the two married on June 15, 1904, in Schuylkill County, PA. The new couple was soon expecting their first child. However, their joy turned tragic when their baby daughter, Virginia, died not long after she was born. A son, Wilbur Clark, came along in 1906, and a second son, Harper Bruce, was born in September of 1907. Now with two children, Abel sought to better his financial position. His uncle, the Honorable Alexander F. Thompson, had been a member of the Dauphin County bar and served as a state senate member. These political connections may have led to

Abel's position as a probationer with the local courts.

By 1910, the couple had been married for six years and was well settled in Porter Township. Schuylkill County would soon be celebrating its centennial and nearby Pottsville was a growing mini-metropolis with ample educational opportunities for neighboring children. Abel had decided to return to the family roots and had been working as a coal miner for eight years. Perhaps the coal miners' strike of 1902, which ended with shorter work days and 10% pay increases after President Theodore Roosevelt's successful arbitration, played a role in Abel taking up mining. Soon, he and Gussie had saved enough to purchase their own home. They were even able to rent space in the household to a small family. Gussie was expecting their fourth child, Abel Franklin, who would be born in October 1910. Their daughter, Lydia Mae, would follow in February four years later.

With a growing family, Abel sensed the increased responsibility that came with it. His job as a miner was fraught with peril—it was all too often he heard of explosions, cave-ins, or exposure to deadly mine gasses. These dangers were impressed upon him by the 1892 explosion at York Farm Colliery—when he was 11 years old—that killed 15 men. The Molly Maguires (a society of activists who fought to improve the dangerous working conditions in the mines) had actively campaigned for better working conditions, but positive changes were still some time off. Violent clashes between organized workers and mine bosses continued throughout Abel's life, from the hanging of twenty Pennsylvania coal miners believed to be members of the Molly Maguires in the 1870s and the Lattimer Massacre in nearby Hazleton in 1897, to the infamous Ludlow Massacre and ensuing Colorado Coalfield War, in which hundreds died in that very year of 1914. Realizing both the apparent and unseen dangers of his profession, Abel took no chances in providing for his family should some ill-fated event occur. He filed his will at the local courthouse in Porter on July 2, 1914.

Abel was obviously pondering the future when he filed his will. Perhaps it was a general sense of foreboding, or maybe he had the feeling that something just wasn't quite right. One of the unseen dangers of a coal miner's life was black lung, always a concern for both current and former miners. Or perhaps it was his plans for an adventurous trip to Colorado. Whatever the case, he was wise to plan well.

Abel heard of the mining booms taking place in Colorado. Family stories say that he left Pennsylvania in search of copper in Colorado. Although copper mines were scarce in Colorado, swindlers like the notorious W. C. Calhoun were not. Abel could have met or heard about Calhoun and the copper mine stocks he was selling. Wanting to provide for his wife and new children, Abel may have left for Colorado to check on his investments; or maybe it was the adventurous spirit instilled in Abel by his grandfather, Alexander, who left Scotland to come to the New World. Upon his arrival in Colorado, Abel found that his stocks were potentially fraudulent and took up employment in one of the many booming gold or silver mines of the time. Gussie, a resourceful woman, was left at home to care for their children.

Abel's trip to Colorado left him feeling rather unwell and he had a strong yearning to return home to familiar soil. Shortly thereafter, he became a victim of the influenza pandemic, and after contracting pneumonia, he died on October 15, 1918. He was just 37 years of age. The leaves had begun to fall, and the Pennsylvania mountains were awash with beauty and color. The family gathered for Abel's burial services on a windswept October day. They said their final goodbyes as he was returned to the soil so near to where his life had begun. His mortal remains were laid to rest in Greenwood Cemetery in Tower City, Pennsylvania.

Abel died leaving Gussie with four small children all under the age of twelve. Rather than choosing to remarry, Gussie decided to brave the world on her own. Luckily, the family home had already been paid for so she and the children had a secure roof over their heads. Gussie's lack of education left her with few options for income, but this did not hinder her in finding a way to earn much-needed funds. With her agile hands, she found plenty of work as a seamstress. This allowed her to remain at home and tend to her children while also supporting the family financially. The boys were still attending school and too young to contribute to the family income, but they managed to persevere and remain together as a family through this trying period of their lives.

In just a decade, Gussie was a financially stable widow living in a community among many other widows. It was a coming new age of amazing technologies. Advances in aviation allowed the imagination to take flight by following the travels and tragedies of Amelia Earhart and Charles Lindbergh. The Jazz age was in full swing, and for a few hard-earned pennies, one could enter the strange and wonderful world of *The Wizard of Oz,* a moving picture show. Gussie was likely amazed at seeing so many things she never could have dreamed of at the turn of the century.

Still the family prevailed as a whole. Gussie was fortunate to be keeping house for her children well away from the Midwestern Dust Bowl and they were lucky enough to be among those who still had jobs at the beginning of the Great Depression. The boys were working as coal miners and Lydia had begun her long-term job as a looper at a hosiery factory. Even for those in a household with multiple incomes, the nation's financial situation dictated frugality in all things. Radio was gaining popularity as an economic American pastime. Like many other families who owned a radio set, Gussie and her children probably spent the evenings listening to their favorite broadcast programs. A pleasant accompaniment would have been a fresh-baked plate of the newly invented Toll House chocolate chip cookies and fresh milk all around.

Several years later, Gussie and Lydia were still living on Main Street in Sheridan. It was a middle-class neighborhood populated mostly by miners and mill workers. Gussie was surely proud to own her home at a value of $680, which would be equal to about $11,315 today. She took care of the house while Lydia worked at the stocking mill. Being the highest paid looper in the area, Lydia earned $550 a year to support them both. It was a modest lifestyle when a loaf of bread cost about 8 cents, a quart of milk averaged 11 cents, and eggs were nearly 27 cents a dozen. With a little more than $10 a month to live on, economizing was a continuing necessity.

While the radio was one of the main leisure activities available, it was also the main means of getting the news. When Germany invaded France and Italy declared war on Britain and France, it no doubt caused them much concern. It was the beginning of a period of unrest that would last for many years. The loss and devastation of WWII may have been the catalyst for Gussie to face her own eventual mortality. She filed her last will and testament at the local courthouse on May 27, 1950, not long after her 65th birthday, at which point she would have started drawing on her Social Security benefits, another innovation of the 20th century.

It would be several more decades before the reading of Gussie's will would come to pass. During that time, she continued to live with and keep house for Lydia, who never married. She continued to find comfort in Lydia's countenance, which reminded her of the dear husband so many years gone. Living through these years, she would see many changes in youth morality, racial discrimination, and in the political face of America. She would experience the loss of her son Wilbur Clark, who left behind a widow, Elva May.

Gussie, an aging widow with a childhood rooted in the Victorian age, took these changes in stride. She occupied her time in charitable efforts as a member of the Women's Society of Christian Service. Finding a commonality amongst other Methodist ladies of similar age and like mind, she spent her days in Bible study fellowship, sharing the gospel with others, aiding the poor, visiting the aged, and assisting those of general misfortune. When she was not on her missions as benefactor, she practiced her faith at the Lykens United Methodist Church or the Wesley United Methodist Church in Tower City. It was a faith that Gussie continued to practice until her passing in March of 1973.

Gussie Hensel Thompson departed this world at the respectable age of eighty-eight years. Her heart and circulatory system failing, she experienced a brain hemorrhage and breathed her last breath peacefully at home on March 27, 1973. It was a chilly day when her loved ones attended her funeral services at the Dean O. Snyder Mortuary in Tower City. There to pay respects were her sons Abel Franklin and wife, Almeda Ellen; Harper Bruce and wife, Myrtle Adeline; and of course, her faithful daughter, Lydia Mae. She was laid to rest next to her beloved Abel in Tower City's historic Greenwood Cemetery. Buried amongst many family and friends, their place of committal is a peaceful memorial garden overlooking a meandering branch of the great Schuylkill River. Abel and Gussie's third child, Harper, was the direct ancestor of the Thompson line.

CHAPTER 2

ROBERT BRUCE THOMPSON
&
LYDIA ANN GOODMAN

ROBERT BRUCE THOMPSON & LYDIA ANN GOODMAN

Named for his grandfather, Robert Bruce Thompson was delivered into this earthly world on September 24, 1847. The family gathered expectantly at their home on York Farm in Pottsville, Schuylkill County, Pennsylvania. The happy expectant parents, Alexander Thompson and Isabelle Stoddart Penman Thompson, eagerly awaited his arrival along with Robert's seven older brothers and sisters, George, Robert, David, William, Elizabeth, Janette, and Alexander. Robert was not the last child to be born to these parents—his younger siblings, Isabelle and James, would later follow.

Robert's early years were spent growing up on York Farm, where his father raised crops. His family was also known to sell coal from the site, which would later become the famous York Farm Colliery. But his carefree childhood existence would soon see many changes. In 1851, at only four years old, Robert would mourn the loss of his mother. It was the same year that Pottsville became the Schuylkill County seat. Three years later, the family would move to a 110-acre farm in the sparsely settled Porter Township area. The farm grew smaller as Robert grew older and the town of Sheridan grew around him. Robert would gain a stepmother when his father took Mary Bast as his new wife. Over the next several years, Robert would be joined by an additional twelve half-siblings as well. He was still living at home and working as a laborer in 1870.

Almost nine years after Robert was born, the Goodman family was expecting the birth of a child. Lydia Ann Goodman arrived on February 20, 1856, and was baptized the very same day. She was the tenth child born to Michael Goodman and his wife, Mary Magdalene Brown Goodman, of Clarks Valley, Dauphin County, Pennsylvania. Lydia grew up on a farm as well. Her youth was uneventful as her older brothers and sisters married and left the nest one by one. By 1870, her brother George was the only sibling remaining at home.

Lydia herself left the parental nest to marry Robert in 1873. She was a delicate young bride at just seventeen years of age. Her sisters Susan and Magdalena were probably on hand to give marital advice to the blushing bride as sisters Sarah and Anna helped Lydia into a crisp white dress accentuated with lace and bows. Dainty earrings adorned her lobes and her soft dark curls framed a face that showed both trepidation and bright expectation. Robert was fashionably dressed in a debonair suit. One could easily imagine the slight smile that played upon his lips as Lydia's brothers, William and John, took him aside for hearty congratulations. Clean shaven, dark hair slightly parted to the side, he faced his new bride with delight. Their wedding took place in Schuylkill County, Pennsylvania, and it was no doubt a grand affair. A jubilant celebration was held with many family members in attendance, including Lydia's brothers, Jacob and George.

Barely settled into married life, the newlywed couple was soon expecting their first child. A son, Benjamin, was born in 1874, but was lost to them in 1875, less than two years later. A second son, Oliver Charles, was born December 13, 1875, bringing a spark of Christmas joy and a measure of comfort for the grieving parents. The couple's only daughter, Laura Louisa, was born in March of 1878. Lydia and Robert were living in Rush Township, Dauphin County, Pennsylvania, when Abel Robert was born on November 28, 1880. Robert was working as a coal miner, probably at the Brookside Colliery in Tower City, where he had been employed for many years. Lydia's parents, Michael and Magdalena, were living next door.

Of course, their lives had not been without tragedy. Two of Robert's older brothers served in the Civil War. Alexander F. Thompson served three enlistments and survived to be a prominent attorney and state senator, but William W. Thompson died in 1862 to disease while serving in the Union Army. Robert's sister Elizabeth died while serving as a nurse during the war and a half-brother, Charles, was lost to a mining accident.

An even more personal tragedy struck in October of 1883, when Lydia and her infant son both passed. Little Franklin Henry was only eight weeks old and Lydia was barely over the age of 27, but age was not a discriminating factor. Without the benefit of hospital care, many new mothers died from complications of deliveries. Puerperal fever, a postpartum infection also known as childbed fever, was a very real threat. During her short life on this earth, Lydia was very well loved. Reverend Arthur Oakes presided with a comforting sermon, as many friends and family gathered close to aid Robert in his time of grief. As Robert was greatly respected, the funeral was the largest in the history of the town. The church overflowed with mourners, and the procession to the cemetery was long. Lydia and Franklin were buried together in Greenwood Cemetery at Tower City, Schuylkill County, Pennsylvania on October 14, 1883.

Even with the support of family and friends, Robert took Lydia's death hard and became very ill. At the time, Robert was a member of the Patriotic Order Sons of America, probably at Washington Post 54 in Tower City. It was a fraternal group whose main goals were to support the public school system and to encourage patriotism and respect for the nation's heritage and Constitution. It was also their purpose to support fellow "brothers" in their hour of need. The group assisted with Lydia's funeral and stood by Robert, which greatly helped in his recovery.

Robert eventually regained his strength and began to rebuild his life. Rising to prominence in the area, Robert had taken a three-year position in the township government as a supervisor, which may have also included duties as a tax collector. He was fortunate enough to find love again with Mary Margaret Moser Uhler, a widow. The two would soon marry and have at least two children together. Their daughter, Agnes Ellen Lenora, was born in September 1888 in Tower City and baptized shortly thereafter. It is possible that they had another daughter named Lillie, but this may have simply been a nickname used by Agnes. Lillie married twice and had several children. She is buried in Greenwood Cemetery with her second husband, Charles Haubenstine. A son, Allen Herbert, was born in January 1891, in Tower City. He served in WWI and was a great source of pride for the family. He died in 1962 and is buried in Greenwood Cemetery along with other Thompson family members.

As if the loss of loved ones through illness and disease were not enough, fate would deal yet another blow to Robert. As he was returning from his job as Porter Township supervisor, his normally docile horse was spooked by a bicycle and bolted. Robert was thrown from his carriage and he sustained a severely broken leg that required hospital care. Had he landed on the other side of the road, he may have been thrown down a steep embankment and killed. It was a narrow escape from death.

Mortal peril would soon strike again. Robert had already lost a son to diphtheria when he himself was struck down by another terrible disease. While just as common and deadly a malady, typhoid fever was often transmitted through contaminated food or drinking water. It would claim Robert on October 10, 1907, one day after the 24th anniversary of Lydia's death. His burial took place in Greenwood Cemetery at Tower City on Sunday, October 13, 1907. With autumn leaves falling like the tears of those bereaved, Robert was finally at rest with his wife and children.

Several of Robert and Lydia's children were still living when Robert passed on. Oliver, who was born in Rush Township, rose to prominence in the community of Tower City. There he became the prosperous owner of the Mansion Hotel. He married Blanche Charlesworth, who was born in 1883 and who would die at age 32 in 1915. Laura Louisa would marry Charles McGough around 1903, and the couple would have several wonderful children. Appreciating the value of family, Laura remained close to her half-brother, Allen, for many years. Abel Robert would marry Augusta Mae "Gussie" Hensel on June 15, 1904. Robert and Gussie would have a short but happy life together. They had five children, four of whom lived to adulthood to carry on the Thompson family legacy, Abel Robert Thompson being the direct-line ancestor.

CHAPTER 3

HOWARD ANDREW CARSON HENSEL & CLARA MATILDA UPDEGROVE

HOWARD HENSEL & CLARA MATILDA UPDEGROVE

In the summer of 1858, the Hensel family welcomed their fourth son and named him Howard Andrew Carson Hensel, after his father. His parents, Andrew Guise Hensel and Catherine Workman Hensel, and his two older brothers, Joseph and Ira, welcomed the new addition with joy and excitement to their home in Wiconisco, Pennsylvania. The eldest son, John Henry William, died as an infant, as was sadly common at the time.

The Reverend William Yose presided over Howard's baptism, and the neighbors and nearby cousins came to welcome the new baby. With three boys born within four years of one another, it was a busy household that would continue to grow. Over the next eight years, four daughters were added to the family: Catherine, Lillian, Clarissa, and Emma filled out a family of eight children.

In 1870, their father, Andrew, worked as a plasterer, helping to keep the ever-increasing number of miners in the region housed. In 1877, mother, Catherine, passed away, leaving the younger members of the family without a mother as they came of age. Howard was eighteen at that time and had likely already been working to help support the family. In 1880, he was still at home working as a laborer, helping his father to support his sisters while also saving for his own future.

In the same year that the Hensels welcomed their youngest daughter, the Updegrove family announced the birth of their second daughter, Clara Matilda, on November 30, 1866, in Lower Ranch Creek, Tremont, Pennsylvania. That December, she was baptized by Reverend Brady and introduced to the community. Her big sister, Anna, about two years old, was particularly proud. Her parents, Daniel Updegrove, a laborer and miner who was originally from Wiconisco, and Sarah Culp, from nearby Union County, would have two more children—William and Nora—in the following years.

Having likely met through one of Howard's co-workers, Howard and Clara took to each other quickly and were married after a brief courtship on his 26th birthday—September 2, 1884—surrounded by family and friends in Wiconisco. Howard's sisters, who were near to Clara's age, were buzzing with excitement for the event. His older brothers came to offer congratulations and advice. Naturally, Clara's sisters, Anna and Nora, were heavily involved in dressing and beautifying the bride. While the white dress had been popularized by Queen Victoria, middle- and working-class brides often chose more practical colors. Clara wore a dark brown and cream-colored dress with neat, modest embroidery and a high neck. This would be her best dress for formal occasions in the coming years. Similarly, Howard's new suit, tailored in dark brown to complement his wife's dress, would serve as his best attire for some time after the ceremony. A joyous wedding was held that Tuesday morning, followed by a wedding breakfast that gave time for congratulations and greetings. The young couple's neighbors wished them luck and fertility, and indeed Howard and Clara were blessed with both.

Clara was seventeen years old when she was married, and not long after her eighteenth birthday, on February 16, 1885, she gave birth to their first child, Augusta Mae, who would be known as "Gussie." The next year brought a son, Arthur. Then came two girls, Helen and Lillian, in 1888 and 1889, respectively. By 1890, Howard had four children to care for, and he had taken up coal mining, perhaps for higher wages than he could earn elsewhere as a laborer at that time. The family continued to grow as Elmer joined them in 1891, and both Myrtle and Clara were born in 1895. A third boy, Victor was born in 1897. The year 1899 brought a daughter, Virginia, into the fold.

At the turn of the century, Howard and Clara had nine children, all less than fifteen years of age. To help make ends meet, the eldest son, Arthur, was chipping in as a day laborer and coal miner at the age of thirteen. The family stepped into the next century boldly, bringing in a final son, Howard, and a final daughter, Edna, in 1902 and 1905. Eleven children made for a home more boisterous and busy than either parent had been brought up in, though only the younger six required much care. By the time Edna was born, the eldest five were old enough to take on jobs and responsibilities in the house to ease the burden on their parents.

At some point, Howard got out of the mines and into working with lumber. Perhaps the frequency of mining accidents, such as the 1892 explosion at nearby York Farm Colliery that killed 15 men, or the periodic unrest over working conditions, or those poor conditions themselves, persuaded him to find a new line of work. By 1910, Howard had moved up to the position of engineer at a planing mill producing finished lumber, and his son Elmer was working at the same place as a carpenter. These jobs were less prone to disruptions in work than coal mining and were better paying as well. Having settled into a steady career as a skilled worker, Howard could look to the next decade with optimism.

By 1915, Howard had become a pillar of the community. Most of his eleven children were grown and beginning their own families, and he had reached the dignity that often comes to a man in his mid-fifties as his gray hair start to show. Similarly, Clara had grown from a blushing teenage bride to a loving grandmother as she approached 50, still youthful but with more pronounced laugh lines. Howard took an active role in the local chapter of the Patriotic Order Sons of America, Washington Camp, encouraging patriotism and supporting public education. In those years of rapid immigration to America, such groups sought to help newcomers embrace their new home. He also accepted a position as deacon for one of the several Methodist parishes in the area, taking part in the spiritual education of his friends and neighbors.

Howard had a calling to save his brothers not only through Sunday services but also through practical action for workplace safety. In the 1920s, Howard branched out to firefighting—first in the coal mines, and later for Bestock Underwear Mills in Tower City, Pennsylvania. In both the mining and the textile industries, fire remained a constant danger. Having a long history of coal mining, Schuylkill County also had a rich history of volunteer firefighting companies to match, including more than 130 organizations over the years.

During the 1920s, Fords buzzed on the streets of the cities to the east and new electric refrigerators hummed in homes while fires roared in Appalachian coal country. The booming postwar economy had prompted the mining industry to expand, digging more and deeper mines and exposing larger than ever numbers of miners to various risks. Poorly ventilated mines were the primary cause as 597 Pennsylvania coal miners died in coal dust explosions during that decade—a larger toll than in the 1910s or 1930s. Larger mines required more non-mining work for safety measures such as ventilation. Consequently, the then-growing union movement continually struggled with the industry over safety provisions, making workers' health a primary concern. It stands to reason that as the nation turned its attention to industrial safety, local community leaders such as Howard were involved with hands-on implementation of important reforms that were needed in these increasingly mechanized workplaces.

In addition to prospering in the postwar economy, the Hensel family had been fortunate when it came to war. Both Howard and Clara's fathers had been mustered during the Civil War, and both returned home safely. Similarly, their luck held out when the States got involved in the First World War. The Hensels' immediate family did not suffer losses, but they undoubtedly were affected by the tragedies that befell their neighbors and friends during the war. They planted their Victory Garden, conserved their resources, and lent aid to their neighbors whose boys went off to war.

Rather, it was the following decade that would trouble the Hensels. Howard and Clara remained engaged as leaders within their community and family until Clara fell ill with cancer in the winter of her 59th year. She would not see her 60th birthday, succumbing on March 28, 1926. She was laid to rest in Greenwood Cemetery, Tower City, Schuylkill County, Pennsylvania, on March 31. Howard—and indeed the entire family— tried their best to adjust to life without the dear wife of 41 years and mother of eleven children. In the way that many lasting marriages end, Howard did not linger long before joining his wife in the afterlife the next year. The cause of death was determined to be arteriosclerosis, but perhaps loneliness was what really ailed his heart when he passed on June 6, 1927, at 68 years of age. On June 9, he was interred alongside his wife in Greenwood Cemetery.

The next generation of the Hensel family would have to weather the difficult years of depression and war that would soon follow without the guidance of their dear parents. While times were often challenging, the family would persevere. At this point, Gussie was a widow, having lost her husband, Abel Robert Thompson, in 1918. She was caring for her younger children and earning money as a seamstress. She likely took over as matron of the family, being the eldest of her generation. Including Gussie's family of five children, Howard and Clara had a total of nineteen grandchildren. Gussie Hensel Thompson's family would carry the Thompson name to the present generation.

CHAPTER 4

ALEXANDER THOMPSON & ISABLLE STODDART PENMAN

ALEXANDER THOMPSON & ISABELLE STODDART PENMAN

A chill October wind mixed salt air with ash from the smokestacks of Edinburgh and carried it up to the farmlands south of the city as the Thompson family gathered to wait for a seventh child to join the clan. Robert Thompson, born June 1771 in Edgehead, and Janet Russell Thompson, born April 1791 in Borthwick, then married for sixteen years, named the boy Alexander upon his birth on October 22, 1805. Alexander was born in Sauchenside Farm, Cranston, Midlothian, Scotland, and was baptized two weeks later on November 3. The older siblings, Christina, Robert, William, Mary, George, and John, ages twelve to one year, quickly took to the new arrival. His sisters, in particular, were expected to help their mother with the younger children. Two younger brothers, John and James, would follow, filling out the family with seven brothers and two sisters.

Edinburgh was growing rapidly in the early nineteenth century, becoming a hub for lawyers and other professionals, and gobbling up nearby land to accommodate its growth. Scottish culture was having its heyday, generating a wealth of philosophy and literature, such as Sir Walter Scott's works of historical fiction. At this time Scotland's capital was known as the "Modern Athens," a place where people of modest birth were afforded the opportunity of rising to wealth and prominence. But the prosperity was not universal, and many poorer Scots sought their fortunes overseas, especially in the growing republic on the far side of the Atlantic.

Alexander Thompson was one of those Scots who found his prospects bleak in his homeland. Despite a quickly growing economy, the population was growing even faster, and competition for work was fierce in 1820s Scotland. As the fifth son in a large family, Alexander could only count on his family to do so much. So he did what many young Scots in his position were doing at the time—he got on a boat headed for America. As was and remains typical of immigrants the world over, Alexander did not take this great journey alone. On the boat with him were his older brother George, George's wife Catherine Penman Thompson, and her younger siblings James, Isabelle, and Robert Penman (aged fifteen, eleven, and two years, respectively). The *Nimrod* landed in New York on July 9, 1827. Having just come of age at 21 years old, Alexander was excited to get a chance in the "land of opportunity."

That opportunity came after a relatively short westward journey, in Middleport, Pennsylvania, where Alexander found work as a teamster, driving wagons loaded with machinery, timber, and other heavy goods. The Appalachian country northwest of Philadelphia was being developed for its ample natural resources, which were needed for the expanding coastal cities. Over the next few years, Alexander became part of the community in Schuylkill County—home to many other recent immigrants—and he obtained his naturalization papers on July 31, 1834. Having become a citizen and having saved scrupulously, Alexander was ready to put down roots and start a family. He bought some land to farm and set his sights on finding a wife.

He didn't have to look very far, as he had already known the girl who would be his wife for several years at least: his sister-in-law's younger sister, Isabelle Stoddart Penman. Isabelle was born on May 9, 1816, in Newbattle, Scotland, the daughter of David Penman, born December 1775 in Gladsmuir and Elizabeth Stoddart, born about 1780. Isabelle joined an already large family with elder siblings Miriam, John, Margaret, Catherine, Elizabeth, Anne, and James. She was eventually joined by two younger brothers, Alexander and Robert, who were four and eight years younger, respectively.

The Penman family was large and industrious, but they unfortunately lost their father at age 51 in 1826, which likely persuaded Catherine Penman Thompson to take her younger siblings with her from Scotland to America. With only one grown son, getting by with so many mouths to feed would have been difficult, so Catherine was doing her widowed mother a great service in taking some of the younger ones into her care. Eventually, their mother would join them in America, and she ended her days in Pottsville, Schuylkill County, Pennsylvania, in 1849.

When the Thompsons and Penmans set off to America, Isabelle was only eleven years old. However, since their journey, Isabelle had grown into a woman and Alexander had taken notice. The pair had a lot in common, from their nationality to common relatives. Also, Isabelle was the eighth child in a family of ten, circumstances quite similar to Alexander's upbringing. Upon her reaching eighteen years, the two were betrothed. The Thompsons and Penmans celebrated New Year's Day 1835 with a wedding in Pottsville, Schuylkill County, Pennsylvania. Isabelle wore a dark green dress with a matching cape, suitable to the cold weather, and Alexander sported a brown coat with tails and green vest. The ceremony was held that morning at George and Catherine Thompson's home, and the new marriage was announced at the Presbyterian congregation the following Sunday.

Over the next fifteen years, Isabelle bore ten children. The first four were boys: George, Robert (who died as a child), David, and William. Two girls followed: Elizabeth and Janet; Alexander F. and Robert Bruce came next; and last, Isabelle and James filled out the household. Motherhood was rewarding in many respects for Isabelle, but it was also a risky affair considering the state of medicine at the time. Not long after James' birth, a house that had been full of children's laughter was quieted by the passing of their mother on April 18, 1851, in Pottsville, Schuylkill County, Pennsylvania. She was buried the next day in the York Farm Burial Grounds.

During his years with Isabelle, Alexander worked the land at York Farm in Schuylkill County, and the children grew and learned to work the land as well. While clearing a field on the farm, Alexander discovered veins of anthracite coal. He began selling the coal, which could be easily collected from the surface. Anthracite coal was prized for its high burning temperature and less foul smoke than that produced by "soft" (bituminous) coal. Later, this land would become the York Farm Colliery, one of the area's major coal mines.

Following Isabelle's death, the family got an infusion of new energy as Alexander married for a second time. Mary Bast, born in 1833, was not much older than the boys, George being only two years her junior. She was the daughter of Isaac Bast and Catharine Kline. The Bast family had eight children: the eldest son, Benneville; five daughters: Floranda, Rose, Mary, Catharine, and Sarah; and two younger sons: Jacob and Charles.

Despite Mary's youth, she was willing and able to take on the challenge of filling in as mother for Alexander's ten children, ages two to eighteen. What's more, she was also ready to mother her own children. That same year, Mary gave birth to the first of another large brood: a boy she named Isaac in honor of her father. The next year brought George (not to be confused with his half-brother George, the eldest of the family). Continuing the family's penchant to reuse names, the next two daughters were christened Isabelle and Mary. The procreation continued as seven more boys were born: John, Andrew, Charles, Abraham, Winfield, William, and Elmer. A final daughter was named Rebecca.

The year after Alexander took Mary as his wife, the Thompsons left York Farm and bought a 110-acre farm in Porter Township, a then-undeveloped section of Schuylkill County. Alexander would later sell plots of this land, which would become the town of Sheridan in 1869. Alexander built a gristmill in 1857, then known as Thompson's mill. The mill was later sold to Grimm & Womer, and then to the Reading Company. The 1850s were prosperous for the Thompsons, as the family's property valuation more than doubled during that decade, from $2,000 to more than $5,000. To put that amount in perspective, $5,000 of assets in 1860 calculates to nearly $2 million in the present day.

While Alexander continued the development of his land, the Civil War broke out and three of his sons were called upon to serve in the Union Army. The family's devotion to the Union can also be seen in Alexander's registration as a Republican, and in the names of the younger sons, Abraham L. and William U.S.G., honoring presidents Lincoln and Grant during their terms in office. While those boys were much too young to serve, the older boys, David, William, and Alexander F., enlisted. William Thompson died at Frederick, Maryland, during his service in 1862. The eldest daughter, Elizabeth, also perished during the war while working as a nurse. David and Alexander F. would return intact from the fighting. Alexander F. served for three enlistments, and he would rise to prominence in the community after working his way through law school, becoming a lawyer and state senator.

During the 1860s and 1870s, Alexander continued to expand his business interests. In addition to his farm and mill, around 1860 he took a position as a superintendent overseeing various properties for Potts & Company, which had established the Potts Colliery just over the county line in Columbia County in 1857. Coal companies often owned most, if not all, of the buildings in the new towns that sprung up around their mines, and having a local person of import oversee their properties would have been helpful.

In 1861, Alexander became the owner of a general store. Between 1865 and 1871, he took contract jobs for mines in the area, apparently buying properties and selling them to coal mining companies—in partnership with his father-in-law—as Bast & Thompson. Thus, Alexander Thompson continued to strive with the same earnestness and character that had earned him a place of distinction in his new home until his retirement in 1871.

Having homesteaded twice, married twice, fathered twenty-one children, and started several successful business ventures, Alexander Thompson no doubt inspired a great many of his friends and neighbors. But he, too, was mortal, and his vigor finally left him at the age of 68. He died on December 4, 1873, in Tower City, Schuylkill County, Pennsylvania, and was laid to rest in Greenwood Cemetery underneath an impressive monument. His son Charles would join him there in 1878. His wife Mary, his junior by 28 years, lived a long life and was finally laid to rest with her husband in 1910 at the age of 76. Alexander Thompson's legacy would continue well beyond his lifespan, shaping the community through his multitudinous progeny and the various commercial interests he had a hand in starting. His son Robert Bruce Thompson is a direct ancestor of the Thompson family line.

CHAPTER 5

MICHAEL GOODMAN & MARY MAGDALENA BROWN

MICHAEL GOODMAN & MARY MAGDALENA BROWN

On a hot summer day, near the steaming banks of the Susquehanna River, John George Gutman and his wife, Susan Brown, welcomed a son. Michael Goodman, born on June 10, 1806, in Lower Mahanoy, Northumberland County, Pennsylvania, was the youngest of four, having elder brothers, Benjamin and Daniel, and a sister. At the age of two, perhaps in anticipation of coming hard times and the death of his father, Michael was taken to live with his grandfather in Berks County, Pennsylvania. The Goodman children would soon be sorrowed by the loss of their mother, Susan, a few years later.

Michael stayed with his grandfather until he was eighteen, when he moved to a farm south of Clarks Valley Road in Dauphin County, Pennsylvania, where he would live out his days. In the next year or so, he was confirmed in the Lutheran congregation at the old log church-school in Schuylkill County, Pennsylvania.

At the age of twenty-four, Michael married Mary Barbara Ramp, who was born about 1805. The couple would bear six children between 1835 and 1846. William, the eldest, would take over the farm and care for his father in his old age. William was followed by two sisters, Susan and Magdalena, then a brother, John. Two more girls, Sarah, known as Sallie; and Catherine, were the last children from this union.

In the 1830s and 1840s, Pennsylvania was the young republic's bread basket. With a climate similar to much of Europe, settlers were able to bring the bulk of their farming knowledge to use in this region, growing fruits and grains from Europe, as well as adopting native plants and techniques. Pennsylvania farmers produced grains, meats, and dairy products, as well as manufactured products such as leather and flaxseed oil. In 1840, more than 77 percent of the 4.8 million employed persons in Pennsylvania were occupied in agriculture.

Mary Barbara unfortunately passed in 1846, likely due to complications from Catherine's birth. After some fifteen years of marriage, Michael—being in his early forties—was now a very eligible widower with many good years left in him. Soon the area matchmakers set to work finding a wife to once again make the farmstead a home.

A woman from the area—who was also older than the usual marrying age—proved to be a suitable match. Mary Magdalena Brown, daughter of Peter Brown and Anna Maria Carl, was a decade Michael's junior, being born in 1816 in Rush, Dauphin County, Pennsylvania. Following the custom that her family had brought from Europe, she went by Magdalena. She was the fifth of eight children, having elder siblings John, Peter, William, and Anna. Her younger siblings were Philip, Rebecca, and Elizabeth. They were grandchildren to Peter Braun, who fought for the British during the Revolution and, interestingly after the War, secured a job working for George Washington. Michael Goodman and Magdalena Brown were married about 1848 in Schuylkill County, Pennsylvania.

Michael and Magdalena had four children. Anna was born later in the same year they were married and two boys, Jacob and George, were to follow. Amid the joys of a new set of births, another tragedy befell the family as Catherine, the youngest child from Michael's first marriage, passed away about 1855, only about nine years old. The family was completed with the birth of Lydia, the last child, in 1856.

During this period, Michael took to working as a carpenter. Since by the 1850s his older sons were teenagers and thus able to take over a large part of the farm work, the head of the household was free to pursue a new craft. Between farming and carpentry, the Goodman family did well in the tumultuous years from 1850 to 1870, increasing their net worth from $1,000 to more than $2,200—more than $600,000 in modern equivalents.

The Goodman farm endured changing times and adapted accordingly. In the middle of the century, railroads were spreading into new regions of the rapidly expanding nation. The railroads brought access to the vast prairies of the Midwest and the Great Plains, and to ever-increasing supplies of grains and meat. The farmers of the east had to adapt to these changing markets. Wheat production was being replaced with milk, butter, hay, potatoes, poultry, eggs, and other products that were needed in the fast-growing urban populations of Philadelphia and Baltimore. This period also saw the early stages of mechanization on farms, as binders and harvesters changed the Northern farm economy and the cotton gin revolutionized the South.

These changes contributed to the growing rift between the regions, eventually exploding into the Civil War. It is likely that John, the second son, enlisted in 1861 at the age of twenty. John was fortunate to return home, marry, and have a family. It appears that this branch of the Goodman family was not fated to grieve for a lost son, as many of their neighbors and relatives were.

After many prosperous years, the 1880s brought the ravages of age to the Goodman family. Michael and Magdalena had enjoyed 36 years together, but again Michael found himself outliving a wife. At the age of 68, Magdalena died on December 17, 1884 in Tower City, Schuylkill, Pennsylvania. She was laid to rest at Zion Public Square Lutheran Cemetery, Tower City, Schuylkill County, Pennsylvania. Michael would not be alone after his second wife's passing; he spent his golden years living on the farm—which had become his son William's livelihood—surrounded by his many children and grandchildren.

In what would be his final summer, Michael Goodman hosted a great gathering of his family on Sunday, August 19, at the farmstead. "The family dinner was spread in bountiful manner under the ancient cherry tree, and a happy feast was enjoyed by all present, numbering 43 persons of the Goodman freundschaft. At the planting of that cherry tree, great grandfather Michael Goodman, who was 94 years of age in June, did not think of such a gathering under its branches, and as the venerable father offered thanks at the dinner table, he expressed the desire that they would all meet at the festal board of Heaven."

Clearly Michael was anticipating the inevitable: he died on December 27, 1900, in Rush, Dauphin County, Pennsylvania. The *West Schuylkill Herald* recorded his passing: "Michael Goodman, the oldest and best-known citizen of this valley, died at the home of his son, William, in Clarks Valley at 3 AM last Thursday morning. His death was due to old age. . . . The deceased was probably the oldest man in the valley, being 94 years, 6 months, and 17 days. He followed farming for a living and retained great vitality up until about a year ago. Up to that time he frequently walked from his home to Williamstown, a distance of four miles. For the past year, however, his health had been failing. He was only bedfast, however, a short time before death overtook him. Early in his life he connected with the Evangelical Church. When the split occurred, he chose the United Evangelical. It is said that for 72 years he was a member and took great delight in church work. The funeral was held Sunday morning. Services were conducted in the U E Church by the pastor, Reverend S N Dissinger, assisted by Reverend C E Hess of Williamstown. Interment was made in the cemetery in this place." Michael Goodman rests in Zion Public Square Lutheran Cemetery, Tower City, Schuylkill County, Pennsylvania.

The Evangelical Church, a predecessor to the modern United Methodist Church, suffered a division in 1894. Nearly a third of the denomination split off and formed the United Evangelical Church, while the remainder was known as the Evangelical Association. United Evangelical members were generally more progressive, favoring the use of English language rather than the traditional German, greater local control, and less authoritarian leadership. The schism was largely about personalities and culture rather than about theology, but it was serious nonetheless. "In some congregations, the controversy divided families, led to verbal and physical attacks, and ended in court battles over the church property. Eventually, or as some have said, 'when enough funerals had taken place,' the factions reunited in 1922 to form the Evangelical Church." Since the secular courts sided with the Evangelical Association regarding ownership of church property, many United Evangelical congregations were starting from the ground up in the 1890's, and thus Michael's leadership in his congregation was likely needed and much appreciated. *The Tower City, Porter Township Centennial* writes:

Michael Goodman was born June 10, 1806, and came to this valley as a young man and was confirmed in the old log church-school in July 1825, according to the old church records. He married Mary Magdalena Brown, a granddaughter of the original Peter Braun. Michael purchased the farm south of the Clark's Valley Road just east of the Dauphin County line and lived there until his death on December 27, 1900, at the grand age of ninety-four. His wife died December 17, 1884, and both are buried in the cemetery in the public square. In his later years, he gave his farm to his son William, who was born November 20, 1835, and died January 30, 1907. He married Christina Hand, a daughter of John Hand, Jr., and they had the following children: Catherine, who first married Lincoln Rhoads and on his death married Herman Niehenke; Ernaline, who married Elwood Showers; Mary, wife of Isaac Thompson; John; Lydia, married Nathan A. Reightler; George; Fayetta, married William Achenbach; Frank; Ellen, wife of William Novinger; and David. John

Goodman married Hannah Houtz and their children were Harry II, Charles E., Golda, and Grace. Harry married Sadie P. Warfield and their child was Helen; Evelyn, married Frank Rosade; Lillian P.; John; Stuart; and Virginia, married J. Robert Hunsicker. Among the children of Ernaline Goodman Showers and her husband were Albert; Charles; Roy; Beulah, married George Schrope; Verna, married Robert Fegley. The children of Charles Showers were Lester; Helen; Anne, married Norman Unger; Violet; and Lawrence. A very pleasant and enjoyable affair was the reunion of the Goodman family, on Sunday, August 19, at the residence of Mr. and Mrs. William Goodman, in Clarks Valley, which is also the birthplace of Mr. Goodman. The following were present: Mrs. Isaac Thompson and children, Paul, Russel and Leona, Sheridan; Mr. and Mrs. Elwood Showers and children, Charles, Beulah, Raymond, Emma, Verna, and Albert, Tower City; Mr. and Mrs. David Goodman and children, Clarence and Elva, Orwin; Mrs. John Goodman and children, Harry, Charles, and Golda, Orwin; Mrs. Wm. Achenbach and children, Harry, Roy, and Frank of Philadelphia; Mrs. Catherine Rhoads and children, Charles, Oscar, Ira, Millie, and Lloyd, Sheridan; Mr. and Mrs. Nathan Rightler and children, Emily and Willie, Tower City; Frank Goodman and son George, Orwin; George Goodman, Clarks Valley; Mr. and Mrs. Wm. Novinger and daughter, Hattie; Tower City. Artist Rowland of Williamstown photographed the group under an old cherry tree planted scores of years ago by great grandfather Michael Goodman, who was also in attendance. The family dinner was spread in bountiful manner under the ancient cherry tree, and a happy feast was enjoyed by all present, numbering 43 persons. At the planting of that cherry tree, great grandfather Michael Goodman, who was 94 years of age in June, did not think of such a gathering under its branches, and as the venerable father offered thanks at the dinner table, he expressed the desire that they would all meet at the festal board of Heaven. May his desires be granted. As the hour arrived for the happy parties to return to their respective homes, all seemed to realize that in the changing scenes of time, another such a gathering might never occur in this world. After 60 years of earthly pilgrimage, Mr. and Mrs. Wm. Goodman were favored by a kind providence in the gathering of all their sons and daughters, with thirty of the grandchildren. It was an occasion of great joy of retrospective glances over the journey of life, and happy anticipations of a reunion in the golden world of eternal deliverance. It was such a day as expressed by the poet:

Scattered o'er various fields by Heaven,
Through various pathways led,
What happiness in peace to meet
Around a common head!
The pleasures of the past recall,
And tell the tales again
It(s) infant dreams, and childhood joys,
And youth's delightful reign,
To plan the schemes of future bliss;
Rejoicing to confess,
That He whose love hath blessed the past
The future, too, will bless.

Michael Goodman's youngest daughter, Lydia Ann Goodman, would marry Robert Bruce Thompson, and their progeny would carry the Thompson name to the present generation.

CHAPTER 6

ANDREW GUISE HENSEL
&
MARY CATHERINE WORKMAN

ANDREW G. HENSEL & MARY A. GUISE

Andrew Guise Hensel was born on February 18, 1831, at home in New Bloomfield, Perry County, Pennsylvania. New Bloomfield is in the central Pennsylvania countryside, west of the Susquehanna River, an area then being rapidly developed for farming and industry. Named after his father, Andrew was the fifth of six children, preceded by his brother John Adam, sister Anna, and brothers John and George. After Andrew came Michael Hensel, who would later become a reverend. Andrew's father was Andrew W. Hensel, a shoemaker, born in Littlestown, near Gettysburg, Adams County, Pennsylvania, and his mother was Mary Guise, born in Northampton County, Pennsylvania.

The Hensel family had been shaped by significant military experience. Andrew W. Hensel served in the War of 1812 as a private. He was among the noncommissioned officers and privates from Captain John McMillan's company, Colonel Fenton's regiment, of the Pennsylvania Militia, who crossed the Niagara into Canada, and also served in Buffalo, New York. The Hensels' military pedigree extended another generation back as well. Both of Andrew's grandfathers, John Casper Hensel and John Adam Guise, served in the American Revolution, in York County, Pennsylvania, under Captain Will, and in Northampton County, Pennsylvania, under Captain Drapper, respectively.

When Andrew went to work, he garnered early experience as a servant, but he soon took up the profession of plasterer, playing a part in the spread of housing that came along with the ongoing expansion of mining in Pennsylvania. The steady influx of miners to the region generated demand in his field, so Andrew was able to enjoy a stable income and confidence in his plans to start a family.

At twenty-two years of age, Andrew would marry Anna Catherine Workman—known as Catherine—on March 17, 1853, amid St. Patrick's Day festivities in Halifax, Dauphin County, Pennsylvania. Never mind that they were married in a Methodist Episcopal congregation. Since most of the early immigrants to America from Ireland were Protestants, the holiday had not yet taken on the Catholic associations that became common in the late 1800s into the twentieth century. Rather, the Americans of the young republic celebrated St. Patrick's Day primarily as an act of anti-colonial solidarity with the Irish in their struggle for freedom from English rule. Since the two families were situated close to one another, it was likely a well-attended wedding, filling the building with friends and relatives on a Thursday morning as the beginnings of spring were just becoming noticeable in the hilly Pennsylvania countryside.

Catherine, the daughter of Joseph Workman and Susan Romberger, was born in Old Lincoln, Dauphin County, Pennsylvania, on May 17, 1838. She was only fourteen years old on her wedding day. Since she was the youngest of nine children, it is likely that economic concerns contributed to her early marriage. This was a common fact of life for the families of the working class at the time. Her sisters, Susan, Nancy, Elizabeth, and Carolina, reassured and advised the girl as the wedding approached and throughout the marriage. Catherine had helped her sisters with their children, so she was aware of the duties and troubles of raising children. And she also knew something of the joy that children brought to a home. Of course, her four older brothers, Jacob, John, Henry, and Joseph, were surely protective of their youngest sister, but the repute of the Hensel family—and the two families' shared military history—may have eased any concerns about the match. Joseph, Catherine's father, served in the War of 1812, and her grandfather Balthasar Romberger and great-grandfather Jacob Lehman both served in the American Revolution in Lancaster County, Pennsylvania.

Soon the Hensel family was growing. Their first son, John, was born in the year they married, but he did not survive infancy. Catherine's pain eased slowly as more sons came quickly. The next year brought Joseph, then Ira two years later, and Howard after another two years. The family's growth slowed as the Civil War broke out and Andrew left home to serve in the Union Army.

In September 1862, Andrew Guise Hensel was mustered into Company F of the 155th Regiment of the Pennsylvania Infantry at Harrisburg. This unit would be attached to the 2nd Brigade, 3rd Division, 5th Army Corps, Army of the Potomac immediately after reaching Washington, where they were held in reserve during the battle of Antietam. Though they did not fight, the soldiers suffered the elements in these early days of the war due to a lack of basic provisions such as tents and uniforms. A great deal of these needs eventually were donated to units in the Army of the Potomac from the soldiers' communities back home. The 155th first fought at the battle of Fredericksburg that December, during which they suffered heavy losses in an unsuccessful series of charges. "Captain Lee Anshultz was mortally wounded, dying the following day, and the color-sergeant, and the entire color guard were shot down." They also witnessed defeat near Chancellorsville, holding defensive positions. The 155th was later assigned to the 2nd Brigade, 2nd Division of the 5th Corps. At the battle of Gettysburg, the 155th was instrumental in the taking of Little Round Top on the second day of fighting, which helped secure the Union Army's defenses. They held that position on the following day, witnessing the final rebel charge from their unchallenged defensive position, and later pursued the retreating enemy.

The battle at Gettysburg helped to shape the unit's identity and likely contributed to the wealth of documentation available on the subject. A succession of injuries leading to honorable discharges among the officers in the wake of that battle led to the promotion of Alfred L. Pearson to Colonel. Pearson and other officers of the 2nd Brigade led these men in learning the tactics of the French Light Infantry and adopted variations of French-style uniforms to match their inspiration. They came to be known as the Zouave Brigade, which included several units of infantry from Pennsylvania and New York, however the trend was more widespread. Units from nearly all of the states on both sides—and the District of Columbia—styled themselves as Zouaves. The Zouaves of the 155th wore a light blue jacket with yellow trimming and tombeaus, or stylized false pockets; baggy blue trousers; and a red sash with matching red fez. They certainly drew a stark contrast with the straight lines and dark blue of the typical Union Army uniform. Subsequently, the unit was attached to various other brigades up until May 1864, when the unit would be reorganized as the 191st Regiment of the Pennsylvania Infantry. Private Hensel was assigned to Company G.

Pearson's Zouaves fought in many other battles and suffered great hardship: in one battle having 83 men killed or wounded in just ten minutes. But they also saw success, and Pearson was promoted to Major General before the war had ended, which happened before their eyes as the white flag was raised just as the Zouaves were heading into the town of Appomattox Court House for another fight.

Victory meant an end to the bitter suffering this unit had witnessed. Over two years and nine months of service, the combined losses for the 155th and 191st Regiments were six officers, 248 enlisted men killed or mortally wounded, and 272 enlisted men lost to disease—not to mention the death and destruction suffered by Confederates and civilians as well. The unit was mustered out at Washington on June 2, 1865, and then welcomed home with a celebration in Pittsburgh, as many of the men had been recruited from that region.

The war years were terrible, but also wondrous for Andrew Hensel as his wife, Catherine, gave him four daughters between 1862 and 1866: Anna Catherine (named after her mother), Lillian, Anna, and Emma. In the postwar years, the sons of the Hensel family went to work in various professions, and continued expansion in the mining industry fueled Andrew's career as a plasterer. Wages in his field appear to have been good enough to raise a large family, though Andrew never accumulated a great deal of wealth.

The bustling Hensel household fell silent in grief as the children lost their mother to untimely death at only 38 years old. Anna Catherine Workman died on February 10, 1877, in Joliett, Schuylkill County, Pennsylvania. She was laid to rest in Calvary United Methodist, Wiconisco, Dauphin County, Pennsylvania. The daughters were still living at home, though at fifteen Lillie was capable of taking on many of her mother's household responsibilities. Howard, the youngest son—then eighteen years old—continued to live at home at least until 1880, working as a laborer to support the younger children.

Eventually Andrew found himself ready to move forward after losing his wife of nearly 24 years. The family would have a stepmother when Andrew married Grace Arrison, though this union produced no children.

In the coming years, Andrew took to working as a mason and also as a school teacher. At the turn of the century, he was living as a boarder, likely exchanging his knowledge and experience for room and board. In 1908, Andrew got ill, diagnosed with Bright's disease, a chronic inflammation of the kidneys. After a sickness of a few months he died at age 77 on December 14, 1908, in Wiconisco, Dauphin County, Pennsylvania. Two days later he was put to rest in Calvary United Methodist Cemetery, Wiconisco, Dauphin County, Pennsylvania. His headstone was adorned with a flag-holder star marked G.A.R. for the Grand Army of the Republic, honoring his service in the Union Army.

A veteran, a father of eight children and grandfather of many, Andrew Guise Hensel lived through great upheavals and the steady pressure of America's industrial development. Andrew's son Howard Andrew Carson Hensel would carry the family line to the present generation.

CHAPTER 7

DANIEL
UPDEGROVE
&
SARAH ANN
CULP

DANIEL UPDEGROVE & SARAH A CULP

Life was hard in the anthracite coal fields of eastern Pennsylvania following the Panic of 1837. Layoffs, wage cuts, and persistently high unemployment afflicted the nation, dooming President Van Buren's re-election campaign. John M. Updegrove, a laborer from Berks County, Pennsylvania—the son of Conrad Updegrove and Maria Elizabeth Angst—and his wife, Elizabeth Reisch—the daughter of Frederick Reisch and Veronica Schmidt—were struggling to keep their growing family fed. The couple had been married for fourteen years when they welcomed their fifth child, Daniel, on June 28, 1839. His siblings Jacob, Catherine, John, and Nancy were excited, but his parents' joy was tempered with worry. By that time, eldest Jacob was old enough to be allowed to work. Though still a child, this would only be a help if there were work to be had. Two more children, Solomon and Rebecca, would come along in the middle of the next decade.

The Updegrove children were afforded basic education, but like most children of the day they also went to work at a young age. As a young man, Daniel became a blacksmith's apprentice, but within a few years he started working as a coal miner. In the 1860s, the coal country of Pennsylvania was in full production, continuously expanding the mines and fueling the Union's war effort.

During the early days of the war, Daniel met and soon married Salome A. Culp, a girl five years his junior, born June 30, 1844, in Union County, Pennsylvania. Her parents, Jacob Culp and Elizabeth Schneck, had one son and five daughters. Salome—commonly called Sarah—and her siblings lost their mother in 1861, while Daniel and Salome were courting. Jacob found his house emptying quickly, but still he was pleased to see his second youngest married at the age of eighteen. The eldest brother, Jonas, who was Daniel's age, respected Daniel and trusted him to care for his little sister. Elizabeth, Henrietta, and Esther advised their younger sibling about her coming role as a wife, and fourteen-year-old Fielta seemed quite taken with Mr. Updegrove. The handsome young man with sandy hair and grey eyes had actually charmed the entire family. On October 9, 1862, there was a wedding at the Culp house, attended by neighbors, friends, and family. The young couple would not have an easy start in their new life, however, as Daniel would soon be enlisted in the war effort.

Inspired by tales of his great-grandfather John Daniel Angst, who volunteered in Berks County and served under Captain Bretz in the American Revolution, several members of the Updegrove family would fight in the war, including Aaron Updegrove, Daniel Updegrove, Henry K. Updegrove, John Updegrove, and Solomon Updegrove.

Daniel and his brother Solomon signed up in July 1863 to fight for the Union. Enlisting in Harrisburg, the two were placed under Captain Edward Savage as privates in the 9th Cavalry, Company B, of the 92nd Regiment Pennsylvania Volunteers. This unit was known as the Lochiel Cavalry. This distinctively named unit's exploits were quite well known even during the war through the regular correspondence of Private George Unkle with the *Daily Evening Express.* The unit saw extensive action in Kentucky and Tennessee, facing off against Confederate cavalry units that had given the Union army trouble in the early phases of the war. Accounts of the Lochiel Cavalry paint a heroic picture of determined men crossing rugged terrain "on half rations, food half cooked, and boots worn off their feet by tramping over the rocks to ease their own good horses, and trusting to Providence to keep down the wide and swift rivers that drain these wild mountains," as they set to destroy key railways and outmaneuver foes.

Standing 5'5", Private Daniel was built well for riding, light enough that his horse would not wear out too quickly. The Updegrove brothers served with honor, surviving many battles. Solomon was struck down in action at Waynesboro, Georgia, on December 4, 1864. This loss pained Daniel for the rest of his days. As a particularly strange coincidence, another Pennsylvania man, Solomon S. Updegrove, who served in the 18th Cavalry, 163rd Regiment, survived the war and went on to become a prominent citizen. This peculiarity likely added to Daniel's grief over his dead brother.

But the war was not yet over, and Daniel's suffering was not quite through. Not long after losing his brother, Daniel was captured and held as a prisoner of war for twenty-one days in Libby

Prison, at Richmond, Virginia. This aged warehouse on the banks of the James River caused the death of many Union soldiers due to illness, exposure, and starvation. The windows were barred but not shut, and the prison was so overcrowded that men covered every bit of floor as they attempted to sleep through their shivering. While some died quickly, others endured for months, even digging an underground tunnel and staging a successful escape. In the largest prison escape of the war, 109 Union POWs made their way single-file through the tunnel. Discovery of the escape was delayed until morning, helping 59 of the inmates to escape safely under the command of Captain Tower and Colonel Davis. Two men drowned in the James River, and 48 were recaptured. Daniel was lucky to only stay there for three weeks before being released, likely when the Union Army overtook Richmond on April 3, 1865. On that day much of the city burned as Confederates attempted to destroy stockpiled goods and the nearly starved populace of the city rioted.

Despite the suffering and uncertainty of the war, Daniel was able to make it home to his wife on occasion. They welcomed a daughter, Anna, in 1864. Another daughter, Clara Matilda, came two years later, followed by William Henry (who died as an infant in 1871), and Nora Jane, born in 1874. With only three surviving children, the Updegrove household was not large for the time, but it was full of activity. Daniel returned to mining after the war and the family subsisted on this moderate livelihood. In 1870, the family claimed $100 in property.

Both Daniel and Sarah had only a few years of schooling, having been pulled away from school to work in their youth. The 1870 census shows that they were able to read but not able to write. However, either through private study or community effort, by the next census the pair were deemed literate. Perhaps the intermittent unemployment due to accidents, labor disputes, and disruptions in the market that was characteristic of a coal miner's life (he had been unemployed for four months in 1880) afforded Daniel sufficient time for self-education.

Hard luck characterized much of Daniel's professional life. In 1887, Daniel lost a lawsuit over some 50 acres of property possessed by Mr. J. M. Blum—upon which much of the town of Williamstown was built—that had been previously owned by Daniel's father, John. John

Updegrove had filed the same claim and lost in 1875, and Daniel was bringing the claim up again following his father's death. Residents of Williamstown were not overly worried, counting the case as a long shot, and indeed Updegrove's case was soon dismissed by the Pennsylvania Supreme Court. At 48 years old, Daniel's prospects for advancement were not bright. He had lost the case and there was little for him to do but continue as a miner.

The Brookside Colliery was one of the most productive coal mines in the world through much of the nineteenth century and into the twentieth century. It was under continual expansion at the tail end of the 1800s, with new slopes being sunk. One of the great challenges of engineering the expansion of mines was providing adequate ventilation. As the mine is expanded, the amount of airflow required to prevent coal dust from accumulating and igniting also increases. This expensive and time-consuming work was a bane of contention between management and labor, as demands for profits versus a safe working environment fueled labor activism. This antagonistic relationship was often rekindled when such an accident would occur. One such tragedy came on May 23, 1899, claiming the life of Daniel Updegrove, who was suffocated by mine gas likely caused by an explosion. He was laid to rest a few days later, on May 28, just short of 60 years old, in Seyberts Lutheran Cemetery in Williamstown, Dauphin County, Pennsylvania.

Daniel would be survived by his wife, Sarah, and their three daughters. Daniel's military pension was a help to the family, but Sarah ended up taking work as a domestic servant to make ends meet. Salome would live to watch the family grow and to help them carry on through hard times, including the growing pains of mechanization in the mines and the similarly mechanized Great War in Europe. Eventually, a recurrent case of carcinoma of the shoulder would bring her to rest at the age of 79. She was reunited with her husband on July 6, 1923, in Seyberts Lutheran Cemetery. Daniel and Sarah's descendants would proliferate in the new century. Clara Matilda Updegrove married Howard Andrew Carson Hensel, and their line continues to the present.

CHAPTER 8

THOMPSON AHNENTAFEL

ANCESTORS OF HARPER BRUCE THOMPSON

1. **Harper Bruce Thompson** (son of Abel Robert Thompson and Augusta "Gussie" Mae Hensel) was born on September 28, 1907 in Sheridan, Schuylkill County, Pennsylvania, USA[1, 2, 3]. He died on July 23, 1981 in Polyclinic Hospital, Harrisburg, Dauphin County, Pennsylvania, USA[2, 3]. He married **Myrtle Adeline Batdorf** (daughter of James "Edward" Batdorf and Beulah Irene Wert) on June 15, 1935 in St. Johns (Hill) Lutheran, Lykens, Dauphin County, Pennsylvania, USA[4, 5]. She was born on January 05, 1918 in Big Run, Dauphin County, Pennsylvania, USA[4, 6]. She died on May 08, 1983 in Polyclinic Hospital, Harrisburg, Dauphin County, Pennsylvania, USA[7, 8].

Harper Bruce Thompson was buried in 1981 in Woodlawn Memorial Gardens, Harrisburg, Dauphin County, Pennsylvania, USA[3]. His cause of death was Cardiorespiratory arrest w/subdural hematoma[2]. He was counted in the census in 1910 in Porter, Schuylkill County, Pennsylvania, USA[9]. He was counted in the census in 1920 in Porter, Schuylkill County, Pennsylvania, USA[10, 11]. He was counted in the census in 1930 in Emmaus, Lehigh County, Pennsylvania(Uncle James Knittle)[12]. He was counted in the census in 1940 in Tower City, Schuylkill County, Pennsylvania, USA[13]. He was educated at School in 1920[14]. He had a medical condition of cardiac arrest due to clot in brain, cataracts, heart disease, hernia. He was employed as a Boxer about Abt. 1929. He was employed as a Lineman (Telephone Co) in 1930[12]. He was employed as a Laborer in 1935. He was employed as a Bell Telephone Co in 1940 in Lineman. He was employed as a Retired mail handler (Harrisburg Post Office) in 1981[3]. He was affiliated with the Lakeside Lutheran Church religion in 1981[3]. He lived in 914 ? St., Emmaus, Lehigh County, Pennsylvania, USA in 1930[12]. He lived in 335 Main St, Tower City, Pennsylvania, USA in 1940[13]. He lived in Harrisburg, Dauphin County, Pennsylvania, USA in 1972[15]. He lived in Beaufort Farms, Camp Curtain, Estherton, Fort Hunter, Harrisburg, Hecktown, Lucknow, Rockville, Uptown, Windsor farms, all Dauphin County, Pennsylvania, USA in 1981[16]. He lived in

2600 Green St., Harrisburg, Dauphin County, Pennsylvania, USA in 1981[2]. His Social Security Number was 205-05-3254[16]. Funeral: 1981 in Jesse H Geigle, 2100 Linglestown Rd.,Harrisburg, Dauphin County, Pennsylvania, USA[3] Political Party: in Republican

Notes for Harper Bruce Thompson:
Harper was named for his grandfather, Robert "Bruce" Thompson.

Funeral of Harper Thompson
Pastor Gregory Harbaugh, John 11:17-44, July 1981
Harper Thompson, 73, died Thursday at Polyclinic Hospital. He was a member of Lakeside Lutheran Church. A former Postal Service employee, Mr. Thompson is survived by his wife Myrtle, and 3 sons Eugene, Gerald and Robert, and 10 grandchildren and 2 great grandchildren. Services will be held…and so on reads the obituary. And that's all it says. But what about the man, the husband, the father, the brother, grandfather and friend? That's the person you and I have known. A tall, rugged-looking man who sometimes cried at movies, who was sensitive to others, and friendly. I only knew Harper for two years, but I won't forget him. Every Sunday when he and Myrtle were in church, I could depend on hearing Harper's deep baritone, 'Hi ya Gregg!' as the tall man walked by and shook my hand. I remember, too, the man in the hospital who got. teary-eyed talking about his sons - 'good sons' he would say; who nearly beamed when Myrtle was near. And who cried when he received communion. You have memories, too. Some fonder than others, I suspect. Some of joy and fun. Others, perhaps, of father angry with erring boys. Of a husband maybe working too hard or worried about bills. Others of Harper's broad smile and great laugh. Of dad playing with his 'boys. You remember, too. That's Harper. For him we grieve. For him we weep. Because we loved him and will miss him. Like Jesus and Lazarus. A good friend. Dead. So he mourned. But the question came "Could not the one who opened the eyes of the blind kept this man from dying?" That's our question too, I think, if we really face up to our grief. "Why couldn't God keep Harper alive and well?" Though death comes to each of us, the timing could usually do better. So we not only weep but we are somewhat angry as well: with hospitals, doctors and a God who didn't seem to help. Yet in the midst of our grief and anger comes a word, a story, of life and hope that overcome death

and sorrow. "I am the resurrection and the life - unbind him and let him go." Lazarus was raised - a sign to John's church that resurrection is not only for the end-time but happens now - in the midst of life and death, joy and sorrow - new life, restored life comes into our world. As we may loosen and let go of the bonds of death and the past. Harper, unlike Lazarus, will not rise and walk among us. Lazarus was for John's church and for us a sign that life overcomes death. We have the sign. Yet not only that. For Jesus' own death and resurrection stand before us - cross and empty tomb - not only as sign but as gift and power. For we, like Harper, who are baptized have taken part in that death and resurrection - washed in it, enlivened through it, "I am the resurrection and the life" said Jesus. Yet he wept and grieved as we do. But death and grief are not final. God has the last word and the last laugh. We are resurrection and life in the midst of Sorrow and death. For God is with us, inseparable from us and Harper. We remember him. And we untie him, to let him go. For us there is life now. There is more to give and to receive. There is time for joy and laughter. We remember Harper. But we also hope - as the communion of saints and in the resurrection of the dead - for nothing, not even death, can separate him or us from God's love in Christ Jesus. I am the resurrection and the life.

Myrtle Adeline Batdorf was baptized on October 11, 1918 in Evangelical Lutheran Circuit, Lykens, Dauphin County, Pennsylvania, USA[5]. She was buried on May 11, 1983 in Woodlawn Memorial Gardens, Harrisburg, Dauphin County, Pennsylvania, USA. Her cause of death was Cardiorespiratory arrest w/ASHD w/pacemaker[8]. She was counted in the census in 1920 in Washington, Dauphin County, Pennsylvania, USA[17]. She was counted in the census in 1930 in Lykens, Dauphin County, Pennsylvania, USA[18]. She was counted in the census in 1940 in Tower City, Schuylkill County, Pennsylvania, USA[13]. She was educated at School in 1930[19]. Her height was 5 ft. 9 in.. She had a medical condition of cardiac arrest due to arteriosclerosis, arthritis, cataracts, diabetes, heart disease, hypertension, obesity. She was employed as a Housewife in 1983[8]. Her estate was probated between May 10-19 1983 in Harrisburg, Dauphin County, Pennsylvania, USA[20]. She was affiliated with the Lakeside Lutheran Church religion in 1983[7, 21]. She lived in Beaufort Farms, Camp Curtain, Estherton, Fort Hunter, Harrisburg,

Hecktown, Lucknow, Rockville, Uptown, Windsor farms, all Dauphin County, Pennsylvania, USA in 1983[22]. She lived in 2660A Green St., Harrisburg, Dauphin County, Pennsylvania, USA in 1983[7, 8]. Her Social Security Number was 165-26-7303[8, 22]. She signed her will on March 30, 1979 in Harrisburg, Dauphin County, Pennsylvania, USA[20]. Funeral: 1983 in Jesse H Geigle, 2100 Linglestown Rd.,Harrisburg, Dauphin County, Pennsylvania, USA[23] Political Party: in Democrat

Notes for Myrtle Adeline Batdorf:
Myrtle was named for her grandmother "Adeline" Row.

Funeral for Myrtle Thompson,
Pastor Gregory Harbaugh, John 11:1-43, May 1983
Myrtle Thompson's death came as a big surprise to me. I'm sure that was true for many of you--especially her family. I was called by Vaughn Miller on Monday morning. The family had asked if I would take care of the funeral services. I said I would and asked who died. 'Myrtle Thompson', he said. The name didn't ring a bell. I thought for a while. 'You took care of her husband's funeral.' Thompson. Harper. Myrtle. I was stunned. I sat down. I had visited her Friday and she was fine. We had a good talk. She had been thinking a lot about her mom, her sons and Harper, with .Mother's Day coming up and all. She shared some stories--and told me her doctor said she was fine but she wanted to lose some weight. She hugged me when I left with the bags she had kept for the Food Pantry. Then on Sunday, I saw Myrtle in church. I was stunned on Monday morning. I liked Myrtle. I will miss her. So will you. A sad Mother's Day for you--Beulah, Gerry, Gene and Bob--for your families, for friends. A sad day--period. We begin to think of the 'what ifs' or the 'might have beens.' I know I do. I think: I might have visited Myrtle more often, to talk. She worried a lot. I might have helped. You probably do the same. Perhaps you are somewhat angry--with yourself; with God for taking her; with Myrtle for leaving so suddenly--and on Mother's Day, no less. Martha was angry with Jesus when Lazarus died. They had called him when their brother became ill. But he had delayed, taken too long. Lazarus died. His friend Jesus--the healer and wonder-worker--had failed him. And Jesus wept. But Martha was angry. Listen to their dialog with some different tones: 'Jesus, where've you been? If you wouldn't have taken so long, Lazarus wouldn't have died. So, why don't you ask God to do

something now.' Jesus replied, 'Martha, you know Lazarus will rise again.' 'Of course I know that--on the last day.' But I'm talking about now! Perhaps not. Perhaps Martha was soft and pious in her sorrow. She went out to meet him though. She was aggressive. Perhaps seeking. I suspect angry. And Jesus accepted the confrontation with care and comfort and strength: 'I am the resurrection and the life; whoever believes in me will live and never die.' Yet Myrtle is dead. We know that. The story of her life for us has come to a sudden close. All we have left are the memories. Yet, a sudden unexpected death was just like Myrtle. I mean, it fits the story. The time I've known Myrtle she's been loving, but tough. Caring but straight forward and painfully honest. She said what she thought and meant it. I always knew where I stood with Myrtle. And she told me stories of how she handled I 'her boys' and how she always told Harper, "You let people use you too much." "I won't put up with that!" Fiercely independent and self-assertive. Even abrupt. But caring--sort of the 'thundering, velvet hand' of Dan Fogleberg's song. Myrtle loved her family deeply. And you loved her and remember her. So, we come together wondering, perhaps, 'where were you Lord?' Sad, angry, hurt. Yet, we recognize that all of us will die, all of our stories, our biographies will end. Lazarus died. But Jesus called him back 'that you may come to believe', he told his disciples. Jesus added a few chapters. And hanged the message. Like the disciples, we look at death as the last reality, the lost fight-of-life, the end. Even when we think in terms of the dead person's soul going to heaven, we have to face the reality that Myrtle is no longer with us--no more talking, or aughing or yelling or threats or love will come from Myrtle. We see death as the end of the story. But the story of Lazarus is a sign for us that the story is not over--'whoever believes in me will never die! That's the promise of Jesus--the one who died and who now lives. Lazarus would die again. Jesus is risen and returned to the Father--forever. I am the way, the truth and the life. No one comes to the Father except by me'. Risen. To give us hope--for life, for living. Yes, Myrtle is dead. But we are not. We remember her life, and we will tell stories about her, and we will live with hope that new chapters will yet be added by our Lord who brings life from death. We are alive--to go from here back to our world--home, school, work, play. Having faced death we can laugh--the laughter of hope and faith in the Lord of life. The laughter of the living. And I remember well that Myrtle really knew how to laugh. I am the resurrection and the life. Whoever believes in me will never die. Amen.

---

2. **Abel Robert Thompson** (son of Robert Bruce Thompson and Lydia Ann Goodman) was born on November 28, 1880 in Sheridan, Schuylkill County, Pennsylvania, USA[24, 25, 26]. He died on October 15, 1918 in Tower City, Schuylkill County, Pennsylvania, USA[24, 27]. He married **Augusta "Gussie" Mae Hensel** (daughter of Howard Andrew Carson Hensel and Clara Matilda Updegrove) on June 15, 1904 in Schuylkill County, Pennsylvania, USA[25].

3. **Augusta "Gussie" Mae Hensel** (daughter of Howard Andrew Carson Hensel and Clara Matilda Updegrove) was born on February 16, 1885 in Wiconisco, Dauphin County, Pennsylvania, USA[25, 28, 29, 30]. She died on March 27, 1973 in Home, Tower City, Schuylkill County, Pennsylvania, USA[28, 29, 31, 32].

Abel Robert Thompson was buried on October 19, 1918 in Greenwood Cemetery, Tower City, Schuylkill County, Pennsylvania, USA[24, 33]. His cause of death was Pneumonia w/influenza[24]. He was counted in the census in 1900 in Porter, Schuylkill County, Pennsylvania, USA(brother Oliver Thompson)[34]. He was counted in the census in 1910 in Porter, Schuylkill County, Pennsylvania, USA[9]. He had a medical condition of Height Tall, Build Medium, Eyes Gray, Hair Dark[26]. He was employed as a Day laborer between 1900-1904[25, 34]. He was employed as a Probationer between 1907-1908. He was employed as a Miner (Coal mines) in 1910[9]. He was employed as a Miner (Colorado) about Abt. 1915. He was employed as a Miner in 1918[24]. He was employed as a Miner (PR CSJ County, West Brookside, Tower City, Schuylkill County, Pennsylvania, USA) on September 15, 1918[26]. His estate was probated between February-November 1919 in Porter Township, Schuylkill County, Pennsylvania, USA[27]. He lived in Wiconisco St., Sheridan, Schuylkill County, Pennsylvania, USA in 1900[34]. He lived in Porter Township, Schuylkill County, Pennsylvania, USA in 1904[25]. He lived in Tower City, Schuylkill County, Pennsylvania, USA in 1918[26]. He signed his will on July 02, 1914 in Porter Tp., Schuylkill County,

Pennsylvania, USA[27, 35]. Funeral: 1918 in John F Dreisingacer, Tower City, Schuylkill County, Pennsylvania, USA[24]

Notes for Abel Robert Thompson:
Abel Robert was named for his father, "Robert" Thompson.

Augusta "Gussie" Mae Hensel was baptized on April 05, 1885 in Dauphin County, Pennsylvania, USA. She was buried on March 30, 1973 in Greenwood Cemetery, Tower City, Schuylkill County, Pennsylvania, USA[28, 29, 31]. Her cause of death was Medullary paralysis w/thrombosis w/cerebral hemorrhage & arteriosclerosis[28]. She was counted in the census in 1900 in Tower City, Schuylkill County, Pennsylvania, USA[36]. She was counted in the census in 1910 in Porter, Schuylkill County, Pennsylvania, USA. She was counted in the census in 1920 in Porter, Schuylkill County, Pennsylvania, USA[14]. She was counted in the census in 1930 in Porter, Schuylkill County, Pennsylvania, USA[37]. She was counted in the census in 1940 in Sheridan, Schuylkill County, Pennsylvania, USA[38]. She was educated at School in 1900[36]. She was employed as a Domestic in 1904[25]. She was employed as a Seamstress (at home) in 1920[14]. She was employed as a Housewife in 1935[4]. She was employed as a Housewife in 1973[28]. She was affiliated with the Lykens United Methodist religion in 1973. She was affiliated with the Wesley United Methodist, Tower City, Pennsylvania, USA religion in 1973[30]. She lived in Tower City, Schuylkill County, Pennsylvania, USA in 1904[25]. She lived in 329 Main St., Sheridan, Schuylkill County, Pennsylvania, USA in 1920[14]. She lived in 329 Main St., Highway Route 199, Sheridan, Schuylkill County, Pennsylvania, USA in 1930[37]. She lived in 34 Main St, Sheridan, Pennsylvania, USA in 1940[38]. She lived in Schuylkill County, Pennsylvania, USA in 1973. She lived in Orwin, Porter, Reinerton, Rush, Sheridan, Tower City, all Schuylkill County, Pennsylvania, USA in 1973[39]. She lived in 329 West Grand Ave., Tower City, Schuylkill County, Pennsylvania, USA17980 in 1973[30, 40]. Her Social Security Number was 173-46-1535[28, 39]. She signed her will on May 27, 1950 in Sheridan, Schuylkill County, Pennsylvania, USA[32]. Funeral: 1973 in Dean O Snyder, 304 E Grand Ave., Tower City, Schuylkill County, Pennsylvania, USA[28, 30, 41] Member: in Member of Women's Society of

Christian Service[42]

Notes for Augusta "Gussie" Mae Hensel:

Augusta "Gussie" Mae Hensel and Abel Robert Thompson had the following children:
       i.   Virginia D Thompson (daughter of Abel Robert Thompson and Augusta "Gussie" Mae Hensel) was born in 1905 in Pennsylvania, USA. She died in 1905.

      ii.   Wilbur Clark Thompson (son of Abel Robert Thompson and Augusta "Gussie" Mae Hensel) was born in 1906 in Pennsylvania, USA. He died in 1963[43]. He married Elva May Matter. She was born in 1911. She died in 1999[43].

1.   iii.   Harper Bruce Thompson (son of Abel Robert Thompson and Augusta "Gussie" Mae Hensel) was born on September 28, 1907 in Sheridan, Schuylkill County, Pennsylvania, USA[1, 2, 3]. He died on July 23, 1981 in Polyclinic Hospital, Harrisburg, Dauphin County, Pennsylvania, USA[2, 3]. He married Myrtle Adeline Batdorf (daughter of James "Edward" Batdorf and Beulah Irene Wert) on June 15, 1935 in St. Johns (Hill) Lutheran, Lykens, Dauphin County, Pennsylvania, USA[4, 5]. She was born on January 05, 1918 in Big Run, Dauphin County, Pennsylvania, USA[4, 6]. She died on May 08, 1983 in Polyclinic Hospital, Harrisburg, Dauphin County, Pennsylvania, USA[7, 8].

     iv.   Abel Franklin Thompson (son of Abel Robert Thompson and Augusta "Gussie" Mae Hensel) was born on October 19, 1910 in Pennsylvania, USA. He died in June 1985 in East Petersburg, Lancaster County, Pennsylvania, USA[44]. He married Almeda Ellen Cox in 1931. She was born in 1911. She died in 1991.

     v.   Lydia Mae Thompson (daughter of Abel Robert Thompson and Augusta "Gussie" Mae Hensel) was born on February

07, 1914 in Sheridan, Schuylkill County, Pennsylvania, USA[45]. She died in January 1983 in Tower City, Schuylkill County, Pennsylvania, USA[43].

<hr>

Generation 3

4.   **Robert Bruce Thompson** (son of Alexander Thompson and Isabelle Stoddart Penman) was born on September 24, 1847 in York Farm Burial Grounds, Pottsville, Schuylkill County, Pennsylvania, USA[46]. He died on October 10, 1907 in Tower City, Schuylkill County, Pennsylvania, USA[46, 47]. He married **Lydia Ann Goodman** (daughter of Michael Goodman and Mary Magdalena Brown) about Abt. 1873 in Schuylkill County, Pennsylvania, USA.

5.   **Lydia Ann Goodman** (daughter of Michael Goodman and Mary Magdalena Brown) was born on February 20, 1856 in Clarks Valley, Dauphin County, Pennsylvania, USA[48]. She died on October 09, 1883 in Tower City, Schuylkill County, Pennsylvania, USA[48, 49, 50].

Robert Bruce Thompson was buried on October 13, 1907 in Greenwood Cemetery, Tower City, Schuylkill County, Pennsylvania, USA[49, 51]. His cause of death was Typhoid fever w/contaminated water[46]. He was counted in the census in 1850 in Norwegian, Schuylkill County, Pennsylvania, USA[52]. He was counted in the census in 1860 in Porter, Schuylkill County, Pennsylvania, USA[53]. He was counted in the census in 1870 in father (Norwegian, Schuylkill County, Pennsylvania, USA[54]). He was counted in the census in 1880 in Rush, Dauphin County, Pennsylvania, USA[55]. He was counted in the census in 1900 in Pottsville, Schuylkill County, Pennsylvania, USA[56]. He was employed as a Laborer in 1870[54]. He was employed as a Coal miner in 1880[55]. He was employed as a Supervisor (Porter Tp) between 1899-1901[49, 56]. He was employed as a Supervisor in 1900[57]. He was employed as a Tax collector about Abt. 1900[49]. He was employed as a Business in 1907[46]. He lived in ? St., Rush, Dauphin County, Pennsylvania, USA in 1880[55]. He lived in Pottsville Hospital, 500 Washington St, Pottsville, Schuylkill County, Pennsylvania, USA in 1900. Funeral: 1907 in John [F] Dreisingacer, Tower City, Schuylkill County, Pennsylvania, USA[46] Member: in Members Sons of America[58]

Notes for Robert Bruce Thompson:
Robert was named for his grandfather "Robert" Thompson.

Robert Thompson, son of Alexander Thompson, was born at York Farm, and died in 1909. During the greater part of his life he was engaged at mine work, being employed for many years at the Brookside colliery, at Tower City. He served three years as supervisor of Porter township, and was looked upon as a citizen of substantial character, deservedly respected by all who knew him. His wife, Lydia (Goodman), died in 1883, and they are buried in the Greenwood cemetery near Tower City. They were the parents of four children: Oliver C.; Laura Louise, who is the wife of Charles McGough, of Frankford, Pa.; Abel, living in Porter township; and Benjamin, who died young. [Schuylkill County, Pennsylvania: genealogy--family history ..., Volume 2 By J.H. Beers & Co]

Robert Thompson, who buried his wife and youngest child last week, is very sick. Robert Thompson of Sheridan lost a two year old boy of Diphtherotic croup. Interment took place on Thursday in Tower City Cemetery. Child by the second wife. Supervisor Robert Thompson is adding a portico to his house in Sheridan. Robert Thompson, of Sheridan, one of the Supervisors of Porter Township, met with an accident while returning home from his day's work on Tuesday, which might have cost him his life. He escaped, however, with a broken leg which will keep him confined to the house for several months to come. On the day of the accident, Mr. Thompson had a force of men at work near Keffers. It was his custom, when working any distance from home, to ride to and from work in a carriage. The horse, of which he is the owner, is kind and gentle and fearless of all things except bicycles. While coming down the State road on the evening of the accident he stopped to converse with a party whom he met. While thus engaged a bicycle and rider came along which frightened the horse who made a plunge, throwing Mr. Thompson out of the buggy to the upper side of the road. Had he fallen on the lower side, he probably would have been thrown down the embankment which might have resulted fatally. After the accident he was taken to his home where Dr. Phillips reduced the fracture which was found to be a bad one, right below the kneecap of the right leg. The injured man is unfortunate in having his legs broken. This is the third or fourth time he has had t o suffer from similar injuries. He was taken to the Pottsville hospital on Wednesday afternoon. [Records of Jim Thompson, jbthompson@compuserve.com]

Lydia Ann Goodman was baptized on February 20, 1856 in Pennsylvania, USA. She was buried on October 14, 1883 in Greenwood Cemetery, Tower City, Schuylkill County, Pennsylvania, USA[49, 59]. Her cause of death was Complications of pregnancy. She was counted in the census in 1860. She was counted in the census in 1870 in Rush, Dauphin County, Pennsylvania, USA[60]. She was counted in the census in 1880 in Rush, Dauphin County, Pennsylvania, USA[61]. She was employed as a Keeping house in 1880[55].

Notes for Lydia Ann Goodman:
Last Sunday Tower City witnessed a very sad, affecting and unusual scene in the funeral of Mrs.. Robert Thompson and her youngest child. Mrs. Thompson was the daughter of M. and M. Goodman of Clarks Valley. She was a young-woman being but twenty-seven years, eight months and eleven days old on the day of her death. The age of her child, Franklin Henry, was eight weeks. It was the largest Sunday funeral in the history of our town, and was under the supervision of the Sons of America, of which order Mr. Thompson is a member. After a short service at the home, a very large concourse of sympathetic friends joined in the mournful procession to the church, which was crowded to the utmost capacity, hundreds being unable to gain admission. Anxious to hear, they thronged the doorway and windows, and with breathless attention, listened to a sermon by the Re v. Arthur Oakes. Subject-"Christ and the power of His resurrection;" Text-Phil. III, 10 -"To know Him and the power of His resurrection." After the sermon in the church, the services were continued in the cemetery, where, amid weeping relatives and sorrowing friends, mother and son, side by side, were lowered in the same grave. They rest in peace, waiting the resurrection morn, when -
The sainted mother shall wake and in her lap
Clasp her dear babe, partner of her grave,
And heritor with her of heaven; a flower

Washed by the blood of Jesus, from the stain
Of native guilt, even in its early bud. [Valley Echo, Tower City, PA,
Records of Jim Thompson, jbthompson@compuserve.com]

Lydia & son Franklin died on same day, October 9, 1883, Tower City,
Pennsylvania [Valley Echo, October 20, 1883]

Lydia Ann Goodman and Robert Bruce Thompson had the following
children:

     i.   Benjamin Thompson (son of Robert Bruce Thompson and
           Lydia Ann Goodman) was born in 1874 in Pennsylvania,
           USA. He died in 1875.

     ii.   Oliver Charles Thompson (son of Robert Bruce Thompson
           and Lydia Ann Goodman) was born in 1875 in
           Pennsylvania, USA. He died in 1918. He married Blanche
           Charlesworth. She was born in 1883 in Pennsylvania,
           USA. He married ?.

     iii. Laura Louisa Thompson (daughter of Robert Bruce
           Thompson and Lydia Ann Goodman) was born in 1878 in
           Pennsylvania, USA. She married Charles John McGough.
           He was born in 1881 in Pennsylvania, USA.

2.   iv. Abel Robert Thompson (son of Robert Bruce Thompson
           and Lydia Ann Goodman) was born on November 28, 1880
           in Sheridan, Schuylkill County, Pennsylvania, USA[24, 25, 26].
           He died on October 15, 1918 in Tower City, Schuylkill
           County, Pennsylvania, USA[24, 27]. He married Augusta
           "Gussie" Mae Hensel (daughter of Howard Andrew Carson
           Hensel and Clara Matilda Updegrove) on June 15, 1904 in
           Schuylkill County, Pennsylvania, USA[25]. She was born on
           February 16, 1885 in Wiconisco, Dauphin County,
           Pennsylvania, USA[25, 28, 29, 30]. She died on March 27, 1973
           in Home, Tower City, Schuylkill County, Pennsylvania,
           USA[28, 29, 31, 32].

     v.   Blanche Thompson (daughter of Robert Bruce Thompson
           and Lydia Ann Goodman) was born in 1883 in
           Pennsylvania, USA. She died in 1915.

     vi. Franklin Henry Thompson (son of Robert Bruce Thompson and Lydia Ann Goodman) was born in 1883 in Pennsylvania, USA. He married Susan Hammer. She was born in 1882 in Pennsylvania, USA.

6.   **Howard Andrew Carson Hensel** (son of Andrew Guise Hensel and Catherine Workman) was born on September 02, 1858 in Wiconisco, Dauphin County, Pennsylvania, USA[62, 63, 64]. He died on June 06, 1927 in Tower City, Schuylkill County, Pennsylvania, USA[62, 63, 64, 65]. He married **Clara Matilda Updegrove** (daughter of Daniel Updegrove and Sarah "Salome" A Culp) on September 02, 1884 in Wiconisco, Dauphin County, Pennsylvania, USA[62, 64].

7.   **Clara Matilda Updegrove** (daughter of Daniel Updegrove and Sarah "Salome" A Culp) was born on November 30, 1866 in Lower Ranch Creek, Tremont, Schuylkill County, Pennsylvania, USA[62, 64]. She died on March 28, 1926 in Tower City, Schuylkill County, Pennsylvania, USA[62, 64, 66].

Howard Andrew Carson Hensel was baptized about Abt. 1858 in Rev. Wm Yose, Dauphin County, Pennsylvania, USA[67]. He was buried on June 09, 1927 in Greenwood Cemetery, Tower City, Schuylkill County, Pennsylvania, USA[62, 63, 68]. His cause of death was Arteriosclerosis[63]. He was counted in the census in 1860 in Porter, Schuylkill County, Pennsylvania, USA[69, 70]. He was counted in the census in 1870 in Wiconisco, Dauphin County, Pennsylvania, USA[71]. He was counted in the census in 1880 in Wiconisco, Dauphin County, Pennsylvania, USA[72]. He was counted in the census in 1900 in Tower City, Schuylkill County, Pennsylvania, USA[36]. He was counted in the census in 1910 in Tower City, Schuylkill County, Pennsylvania, USA[73]. He was counted in the census in 1920 in Tower City, Schuylkill County, Pennsylvania, USA[74]. He was employed as a Laborer in 1880[75]. He was employed as a Coal miner in 1900[36]. He was employed as a Engineer (P? Mill) in 1910[73]. He was employed as a Deacon (Methodist) about Abt. 1915[64]. He was employed as a Fireman (Coal mine) in 1920[74]. He was employed as a Fireman (Bestock Underwear Mills, Tower City, Pennsylvania, USA) in 1927[63]. He lived in Wiconisco Ave., Tower City, Schuylkill County, Pennsylvania, USA between 1910-1920[73, 76]. He lived in Hand &

Wiconisco Aves., Tower City, Schuylkill County, Pennsylvania, USA in 1927[64, 65]. He signed his will on January 17, 1918 in Tower City, Schuylkill County, Pennsylvania, USA[65]. Funeral: 1927 in Duane Snyder, 304 E Grand Ave., Tower City, Schuylkill County, Pennsylvania, USA[63] Member: in Member Patriotic Order of Sons of America[77]

Notes for Howard Andrew Carson Hensel:
Howard Andrew was named for his father "Andrew" G Hensel.

Clara Matilda Updegrove was baptized in December 1866 in Rev. Brady, Schuylkill County, Pennsylvania, USA[64, 67]. She was buried on March 31, 1926 in Greenwood Cemetery, Tower City, Schuylkill County, Pennsylvania, USA[62, 66, 78]. Her cause of death was Metastatic carcinoma of medial atrium & left chest w/carcinoma breast[66]. She was counted in the census in 1870 in Williamstown, Dauphin County, Pennsylvania, USA[79]. She was counted in the census in 1880 in Williamstown, Dauphin County, Pennsylvania, USA[80]. She was counted in the census in 1900 in Tower City, Schuylkill County, Pennsylvania, USA. She was counted in the census in 1910 in Tower City, Schuylkill County, Pennsylvania, USA. She was counted in the census in 1920 in Tower City, Schuylkill County, Pennsylvania, USA. She was employed as a Housewife in 1926[66]. Funeral: 1926 in Duane Snyder, 304 E Grand Ave., Tower City, Schuylkill County, Pennsylvania, USA[66]

Clara Matilda Updegrove and Howard Andrew Carson Hensel had the following children:

3.　　i.　Augusta "Gussie" Mae Hensel (daughter of Howard Andrew Carson Hensel and Clara Matilda Updegrove) was born on February 16, 1885 in Wiconisco, Dauphin County, Pennsylvania, USA[25, 28, 29, 30]. She died on March 27, 1973 in Home, Tower City, Schuylkill County, Pennsylvania, USA[28, 29, 31, 32]. She married Abel Robert Thompson (son of Robert Bruce Thompson and Lydia Ann Goodman) on June 15, 1904 in Schuylkill County, Pennsylvania, USA[25].

He was born on November 28, 1880 in Sheridan, Schuylkill County, Pennsylvania, USA[24, 25, 26]. He died on October 15, 1918 in Tower City, Schuylkill County, Pennsylvania, USA[24, 27].

ii. Arthur Preston Hensel (son of Howard Andrew Carson Hensel and Clara Matilda Updegrove) was born in 1886 in Dayton, Dauphin County, Pennsylvania, USA. He died in 1928. He married Lavinia Eva White. She was born in 1890 in Pennsylvania, USA. He married Catherine Sterner. She was born in 1890.

iii. Helen Irene Hensel (daughter of Howard Andrew Carson Hensel and Clara Matilda Updegrove) was born in 1888 in Pennsylvania, USA. She married Edgar Isaiah Artz. He was born in 1878. He died in 1906.

iv. Lillian "Lillie" Verna Hensel (daughter of Howard Andrew Carson Hensel and Clara Matilda Updegrove) was born in 1889 in Pennsylvania, USA. She married John F Yohe. He was born in 1887. He died in 1907.

v. Elmer Elsworth Hensel (son of Howard Andrew Carson Hensel and Clara Matilda Updegrove) was born in 1891 in Pennsylvania, USA. He married Loretta Semrow. She was born in 1900 in wl. She died in 1933[81].

vi. Myrtle Willene Hensel (daughter of Howard Andrew Carson Hensel and Clara Matilda Updegrove) was born in 1895 in Pennsylvania, USA. She married Harry E Sterner. He was born in 1890.

vii. Clara Viola Hensel (daughter of Howard Andrew Carson Hensel and Clara Matilda Updegrove) was born in 1895 in Pennsylvania, USA. She married Harper A Underkoffler. He was born in 1894 in Pennsylvania, USA.

viii. Victor Daniel Hensel (son of Howard Andrew Carson Hensel and Clara Matilda Updegrove) was born in 1897 in Pennsylvania, USA. He married Esther C Craig. She was born in 1898 in Pennsylvania, USA.

ix. Virginia Verogne Hensel (daughter of Howard Andrew Carson Hensel and Clara Matilda Updegrove) was born in 1899 in Pennsylvania, USA. She married Amos C Houtz. He was born in 1904.

x. Howard Alfred Hensel (son of Howard Andrew Carson Hensel and Clara Matilda Updegrove) was born in 1902 in Pennsylvania, USA.

xi. Edna Boyer Hensel (daughter of Howard Andrew Carson Hensel and Clara Matilda Updegrove) was born on March 30, 1905 in Pennsylvania, USA. She died on October 14, 2001 in Allentown, Lehigh County, Pennsylvania, USA. She married James E Knittle. He was born in 1900.

Generation 4

8. **Alexander Thompson** (son of Robert Thompson and Janet Russell) was born on October 22, 1805 in Sauchenside Farm, Cranston, Midlothian, Scotland[82, 83, 84, 85]. He died on December 04, 1873 in Tower City, Schuylkill County, Pennsylvania, USA[61, 86, 87]. He married **Isabelle Stoddart Penman** (daughter of David Penman and Elizabeth Stoddart) on January 01, 1835 in Pottsville, Schuylkill County, Pennsylvania, USA[82].

9. **Isabelle Stoddart Penman** (daughter of David Penman and Elizabeth Stoddart) was born on May 09, 1816 in Newbattle, Midlothian, Scotland[61]. She died on April 18, 1851 in Pottsville, Schuylkill County, Pennsylvania, USA[88].

Alexander Thompson was baptized on November 03, 1805 in Cranston, Midlothian, Scotland[83]. He was buried in December 1873 in Greenwood Cemetery, Tower City, Schuylkill County, Pennsylvania, USA[86, 89]. He was counted in the census in 1830. He was counted in the census in 1840 in Norwegian, Schuylkill County, Pennsylvania, USA[90]. He was counted in the census in 1850 in Norwegian, Schuylkill County, Pennsylvania, USA[52]. He was counted in the census in 1860 in Porter, Schuylkill County, Pennsylvania, USA[53]. He was counted in the census in 1870 in Norwegian, Schuylkill County, Pennsylvania, USA[54]. He immigrated to Scotland to New York, NY (ship Nimrod) on July 09, 1827[91, 92]. He was naturalized on July 31, 1834 in Schuylkill County, Pennsylvania, USA[93, 94]. He was employed as a Farming in 1850[52]. He was employed as a Laid out town of Sheridan, Pennsylvania, USA in 1854[86]. He was employed as a Farmer in 1860[53]. He was employed as a Superintendent (Potts & Co) about Abt. 1860[95]. He was employed as a Owner general store between 1861-1873[96]. He was employed as a Contract work (Mines) between 1865-1871[95]. He was employed as a Laborer in 1870[54]. He was employed as a Colliery owner[83]. He was employed as a Teamster[83]. His estate was probated on December 17, 1873 in Porter Township, Schuylkill County, Pennsylvania, USA[97]. His estate was probated on January 25, 1912 in Porter Township, Schuylkill County, Pennsylvania, USA(after Mary Thompson's death)[97]. He lived in Middleport, Schuylkill County, Pennsylvania, USA about Abt. 1827[86]. He lived in York Farm Burial Grounds, Pottsville, Schuylkill County, Pennsylvania, USA after Aft. 1828[86]. He lived in Porter, Schuylkill County, Pennsylvania, USA in 1854[86]. He lived in Alexander Thompson Homestead. He signed his will on December 03, 1873 in Porter Township, Schuylkill County, Pennsylvania, USA[97]. Political Party: in Republican[98]

Notes for Alexander Thompson:
Alexander Thompson was a native of Scotland, and came to this country during his young manhood. The rest of his life was spent in Schuylkill county, Pa., where he was widely and favorably known during his active, useful career. He first settled at Middleport, where he was engaged in hauling machinery, timber, etc., and later lived at the York Farm, near Pottsville, which he bought, cultivating that tract for many years. He also had small drifts opened on the property and sold coal to the public, this being the first coal taken from the workings later developed into the famous York Farm colliery. After a long residence there he removed to Porter Township, in 1854, being one of the early settlers in this section, where he bought a farm of no acres, from which he subsequently sold a number of building lots for the town of Sharadin [Sheridan], which was laid out in 1869. This was his home until his death, which occurred Dec. 4, 1873; he is buried in the Greenwood cemetery in Porter Township. Besides farming, Mr. Thompson also engaged in milling in Porter Township, building a gristmill upon his tract which was known in his day as Thompson's

mill. It was sold to Grimm & Womer, and later to the Reading Company, the present owners of the land. Mr. Thompson was a man of intelligence and strong character, and in his day was one of the most influential men in this section. By his first marriage, to Isabella Pennman, Mr. Thompson had nine children: George was killed at York Farm; David P., deceased, was a soldier in the Civil war; Elizabeth, deceased, was the wife of Hiram Kimmel; Janette married Benjamin Houtz; William died while serving in the Civil war; Alexander is living at Lykens, Pa.; Robert is deceased; Isabella is the widow of George Powell; James is living in West Virginia. For his second wife Mr. Thompson married Mary Bast, daughter of Isaac Bast, and by this union there was also a large family: Isaac B.; George, who is now living in Alaska; Mary, wife of Daniel Stout; John, residing at Sharadin, Pa.; Andrew, a resident of Michigan; Charles, deceased; Abraham, deceased; Winfield S., of Michigan; William U. S. G., deceased; Elmer E., of Sharadin; and Rebecca M., wife of Hoplin Evans, living on the old Thompson homestead in Porter township. [Schuylkill County, Pennsylvania, By J.H. Beers & Co, Beers (J. H.) and Company]

Go to History of Schuylkill Co for more info:
http://www.rootsweb.com/~usgenweb/pa/schuylkill/pdf/munsell.pdf

Isabelle Stoddart Penman was buried on April 19, 1851 in York Farm Burial Grounds, Pottsville, Schuylkill County, Pennsylvania, USA[99]. She was counted in the census in 1830. She was counted in the census in 1840 in husband (Norwegian, Schuylkill County, Pennsylvania, USA). She was counted in the census in 1850 in Norwegian, Schuylkill County, Pennsylvania, USA. She immigrated in 1828[100]. She was employed as a Homemaker about Abt. 1840.

Isabelle Stoddart Penman and Alexander Thompson had the following children:

  i.   George Thompson (son of Alexander Thompson and Isabelle Stoddart Penman) was born in 1835 in Pennsylvania, USA.

  ii. Robert Thompson (son of Alexander Thompson and Isabelle Stoddart Penman) was born in 1836 in

Pennsylvania, USA. He married Helen ?.

iii. David Penman Thompson (son of Alexander Thompson and Isabelle Stoddart Penman) was born in 1837 in Pennsylvania, USA. He died in 1912. He married "Cassie" Houtz. She was born in 1841 in Pennsylvania, USA. She died in 1883.

iv. William W Thompson (son of Alexander Thompson and Isabelle Stoddart Penman) was born in 1839 in Pennsylvania, USA. He married Mary A ?. She was born in 1836 in Pennsylvania, USA.

v. Elizabeth Thompson (daughter of Alexander Thompson and Isabelle Stoddart Penman) was born in 1841 in Pennsylvania, USA. She married Hiram Kimmel.

vi. Janet "Jennie" Thompson (daughter of Alexander Thompson and Isabelle Stoddart Penman) was born in 1844 in Pennsylvania, USA. She married Benjamin Houtz.

vii. Alexander F Thompson (son of Alexander Thompson and Isabelle Stoddart Penman) was born in 1845 in Pennsylvania, USA. He married Elizabeth Hawk. He married Mary A ?. She was born in 1867 in Pennsylvania, USA.

4. viii. Robert Bruce Thompson (son of Alexander Thompson and Isabelle Stoddart Penman) was born on September 24, 1847 in York Farm Burial Grounds, Pottsville, Schuylkill County, Pennsylvania, USA[46]. He died on October 10, 1907 in Tower City, Schuylkill County, Pennsylvania, USA[46, 47]. He married Lydia Ann Goodman (daughter of Michael Goodman and Mary Magdalena Brown) about Abt. 1873 in Schuylkill County, Pennsylvania, USA. She was born on February 20, 1856 in Clarks Valley, Dauphin County, Pennsylvania, USA[48]. She died on October 09, 1883 in Tower City, Schuylkill County, Pennsylvania, USA[48, 49, 50]. He married Mary Margaret Moser about Abt. 1885. She was born in 1850.

ix. Isabelle Penman Thompson (daughter of Alexander Thompson and Isabelle Stoddart Penman) was born in 1849 in Pennsylvania, USA. She died in 1918. She married George Powell.

x. James C Thompson (son of Alexander Thompson and Isabelle Stoddart Penman) was born in 1851 in Pennsylvania, USA.

10. **Michael Goodman** (son of John George Gutman and ? Brown) was born on June 10, 1806 in Lower Mahanoy Northumberland County, Pennsylvania, USA[101, 102, 103]. He died on December 27, 1900 in Rush, Dauphin County, Pennsylvania, USA[101, 104]. He married **Mary Magdalena Brown** (daughter of Peter Braun Brown and Anna Maria ?) about Abt. 1849 in Schuylkill County, Pennsylvania, USA.

11. **Mary Magdalena Brown** (daughter of Peter Braun Brown and Anna Maria ?) was born in 1816 in Rush, Dauphin Co., ,Pennsylvania. She died on December 17, 1884 in Tower City, Schuylkill, Pennsylvania[101].

Michael Goodman was buried in 1900 in Zion (Public Square) Lutheran Cemetery, Tower City, Schuylkill County, Pennsylvania, USA[104]. His cause of death was Old age[104]. He was counted in the census in 1810 (w/grandfather). He was counted in the census in 1820 (w/grandfather). He was counted in the census in 1830. He was counted in the census in 1840 in Lower Mahantango, Schuylkill County, Pennsylvania, USA[105]. He was counted in the census in 1850 in Rush, Dauphin County, Pennsylvania, USA[106]. He was counted in the census in 1860 in Rush, Dauphin County, Pennsylvania, USA[107]. He was counted in the census in 1870 in Rush, Dauphin County, Pennsylvania, USA[60]. He was counted in the census in 1880 in Rush, Dauphin County, Pennsylvania, USA[108]. He was counted in the census in 1900 in Rush, Dauphin County, Pennsylvania, USA(son William Goodman)[109]. He was confirmed in July 1825 in Schuylkill County, Pennsylvania, USA[101, 110]. He was employed as a Carpenter in 1850[111]. He was employed as a Farmer between 1860-1880[60, 112, 113]. He was employed as a Retired in 1900[109]. He was employed as a Farmer in 1901[104]. His estate was probated on January 11, 1901 in

Rush Township, Dauphin County, Pennsylvania, USA(listed in index only)[114]. He was affiliated with the United Evangelical[102] religion. He lived in Berks County, Pennsylvania, USA in 1808[102]. He lived in Dauphin County, Pennsylvania, USA in 1824[102].

Notes for Michael Goodman:
Michael Guteman was born June 10, 1806 and came to this valley as a young man and was confirmed in the old log church-school in July 1825, according to the old church records. He married Mary Magdalena Brown, a granddaughter of the original Peter Braun. Michael purchased the farm south of the Clark's Valley Road just east of the Dauphin County line and lived there until his death on December 27, 1900 at the grand age of ninety-four. His wife died December 17, 1884 and both are buried in the cemetery in the public square. In his later years he gave his farm to his son, William, who was born November 20, 1835, and died January 30, 1907. He married Christina Hand, a daughter of John Hand, Jr. and they had the follow in g children: Catherine, who first married Lincoln Rhoads and on his death married Herman Niehenke; Ernaline, who married Elwood Showers; Mary, wife of Isaac Thompson; John; Lydia, married Nathan A. Reightler; George; Fayetta, married William Achenbach; Frank; Ellen, wife of William Novinger and David. John Goodman married Hannah Houtz and their children were Harry II, Charles E., Golda and Grace. Harry married Sadie P. Warfield and their children were Helen; Evelyn, married Frank Rosade; Lillian P.; John; Stuart and Virginia, married J. Robert Hunsicker. Among the children of Ernaline Goodman Showers and her husband were Albert; Charles; Roy; Beulah, married George Schrope; Verna, married Robert Fegley. The children of Charles Showers were Lester; Helen; Anne, married Norman Unger; Violet and Lawrence. [Records of Jim Thompson, jbthompson@compuserve.com]

Michael Goodman, the oldest and best known citizen of this valley, died at the home of his son, William, in Clarks Valley at 3 AM last Thursday morning. His death was due to old age. The deceased was born June 10, 1806 in Northumberland County. When nearly two years old, his mother took him to Berks County, where he remained with his grandfather until 18 years of age. At that age he came to this valley, locating on a farm in Clark's Valley where he resided up until the time of his death. The deceased was probably the oldest man in the valley, being 94 years, 6 months and 17 days. He followed farming for a living and retained great vitality up until about a year ago. Up to that time he frequently walked from his home to Williamstown, a distance of four miles. For the past year, however, his health had been failing. He was only bedfast, however, a short time before death overtook him. Early in his life he connected with the Evangelical church. When the split occurred, he chose the United Evangelical. It is said that for 72 years he was a member and took great delight in church work. The funeral was held Sunday morning. Services were conducted in the U E Church by the pastor, Reverend S N Dissinger, assisted by Reverend C E Hess of Williamstown. Interment was made in the cemetery in this place. [FROM 'THE WEST SCHUYLKILL HERALD', 03 JANUARY 1901, Jeffrey A. Brown, ntrprz@dmv.com]

A very pleasant and enjoyable affair was the reunion of the Goodman family, on Sunday, August 19th, at the residence of Mr. And Mrs. William Goodman, in Clarks Valley, which is also the birthplace of Mr. Goodman. The following were present: -- Mrs. Isaac Thompson and children, Paul, Russel and Leona, Sheridan; Mr. And Mrs. Elwood Showers and children, Charles, Beulah, Raymond, Emma, Verna and Albert, Tower City; Mr. And Mrs. David Goodman and children, Clarence and Elva, Orwin; Mrs.. John Goodman and children, Harry, Charles and Golda, Orwin; Mrs. Wm. Achenbach and children, Harry, Roy and Frank of Phila.; Mrs. Catherine Rhoads and children, Charles, Oscar, Ira, Millie and Lloyd, Sheridan; Mr. And Mrs. Nathan Rightler and children, Emily and Willie, Tower City; Frank Goodman and son George, Orwin; George Goodman, Clarks Valley; Mr. an d Mrs. Wm. Novinger and daughter Hattie, Tower City. Artist Rowland of Williamstown, photographed the group under an old cherry tree planted scores of years ago by great grandfather Michael Goodman, who was also in attendance. The family dinner was spread in bountiful manner under the ancient cherry tree, and a happy feast was enjoyed by all present, numbering 43 persons of the Goodman freund-schaft. At the planting of that cherry tree, great grandfather, Michael Goodman, who was 94 years of age in June, did not think of such a gathering under its branches, and as the venerable father offered thanks at the dinner table, he expressed the desire that they would all meet at the festal board of Heaven. May his desires be granted. As the hour arrived for the happy parties to return to their respective homes, all seemed to realize that in the changing scenes of time, another such a gathering might never occur in this world. After 60 years of earthly pilgrimage, Mr. and Mrs. Wm. Goodman, were favored by a kind providence in the gathering of all their sons and daughters, with thirty of the grandchildren. It was an occasion of great joy of retrospective glances over the journey of life, and happy anticipations of a reunion in the golden world of eternal deliverance. It was such a day as expressed by the poet:

Scattered o'er various fields by Heaven,
Through various pathways led,
What happiness in peace to meet
Around a common head!
The pleasures of the past recall,
And tell the tales again
It(s) infant dreams, and childhood joys,
And youth's delightful reign,
To plan the schemes of future bliss;
Rejoicing to confess,
That He whose love hath blessed the past
The future, too, will bless.
[Tower City, Porter Township Centennial book, 1868-1968, Records of Jim Thompson, jbthompson@compuserve.com]

Mary Magdalena Brown was buried in 1884 in Zion (Public Square) Lutheran Cemetery, Tower City, Schuylkill County, Pennsylvania, USA. She was counted in the census in 1820 in Rush, Dauphin County, Pennsylvania, USA ((unlisted)[115]). She was counted in the census in 1830 in Rush, Dauphin County, Pennsylvania, USA (w/father[116]). She was counted in the census in 1840 in Lower Mahantango, Schuylkill County, Pennsylvania, USA (w/husband). She was counted in the census in 1850 in Rush, Dauphin County, Pennsylvania, USA. She was counted in the census in 1860 in Rush, Dauphin County, Pennsylvania, USA ((Margaret)). She was counted in the census in 1870 in Rush, Dauphin County, Pennsylvania, USA[117]. She was counted in the census in 1880 in Rush, Dauphin County, Pennsylvania, USA. She was employed as a Keeping house between 1870-1880[108, 117].

Notes for Mary Magdalena Brown:
Mary was named after her mother "Maria" ?.

Mary Magdalena Brown and Michael Goodman had the following children:

    i.   Jacob Goodman (son of Michael Goodman and Mary Magdalena Brown) was born in 1850 in Pennsylvania, USA.

    ii.   George H Goodman (son of Michael Goodman and Mary Magdalena Brown) was born in 1853 in Pennsylvania, USA. He married Mary ?. She was born in 1860 in Pennsylvania, USA.

5.   iii.   Lydia Ann Goodman (daughter of Michael Goodman and Mary Magdalena Brown) was born on February 20, 1856 in Clarks Valley, Dauphin County, Pennsylvania, USA[48]. She died on October 09, 1883 in Tower City, Schuylkill County, Pennsylvania, USA[48, 49, 50]. She married Robert Bruce Thompson (son of Alexander Thompson and Isabelle Stoddart Penman) about Abt. 1873 in Schuylkill County, Pennsylvania, USA. He was born on September 24, 1847 in York Farm Burial Grounds, Pottsville, Schuylkill County, Pennsylvania, USA[46]. He died on October 10, 1907 in Tower City, Schuylkill County, Pennsylvania, USA[46, 47].

12.   **Andrew Guise Hensel** (son of Andrew W Hensel and Mary A Guise) was born on February 18, 1831 in Home, New Bloomfield, Perry County, Pennsylvania, USA[62, 118, 119, 120]. He died on December 14, 1908 in Wiconisco, Dauphin County, Pennsylvania, USA[62, 121]. He married **Catherine Workman** (daughter of Joseph Workman and Susan Romberger) on May 17, 1853 in Halifax, Dauphin County, Pennsylvania, USA[118, 119].

13.   **Catherine Workman** (daughter of Joseph Workman and Susan Romberger) was born on May 17, 1838 in Old Lincoln, Dauphin County, Pennsylvania, USA[62]. She died on February 10, 1877 in Joliett, Schuylkill County, Pennsylvania, USA[62].

Andrew Guise Hensel was born on February 20, 1832 in Pennsylvania, USA[122]. He was buried on December 16, 1908 in Calvary United Methodist, Wiconisco, Dauphin County, Pennsylvania, USA[62]. His cause of death was Bright's disease (ie, Chronic inflammation of kidneys) w/old age[121]. He was counted in the census in 1840 in Centre, Perry County, Pennsylvania, USA (w/father[123]). He was counted in the census in 1850 in Centre, Perry County, Pennsylvania, USA[124]. He was counted in the census in 1860 in Porter, Schuylkill County, Pennsylvania, USA ((Hentzel)[70, 125]). He was counted in the census in 1870 in Wiconisco, Dauphin County, Pennsylvania, USA[71, 126]. He was counted in the census in 1880 in Wiconisco, Dauphin County, Pennsylvania, USA[127]. He was counted in the census in 1900 in Wiconisco, Dauphin County, Pennsylvania, USA ((Weist-Heheel)[128]). He served in the military on August 28, 1864 in Pittsburgh) (Civil War, Private, 155th Reg Pennsylvania, USA Inf, Co F (Harrisburg[129, 130]). He served in the military on June 02, 1865 (Civil War, Private, 191st Reg Pennsylvania, USA Inf, Co G (organized in fields)[131, 132]). He was employed as a Plasterer between 1850-1900[75, 124, 133, 134, 135]. He was employed as a Servant about Abt. 1850. He was employed as a Plasterer in 1853[118, 119]. He was employed as a Boarder in 1900[136]. He was employed as a Mason & School teacher in 1908[121]. He was affiliated with the Methodist Episcopal religion in 1853[118]. Funeral: 1908 in John Reiff, Lykens, Dauphin County, Pennsylvania, USA[121]

Notes for Andrew Guise Hensel:
Andrew was named after his father "Andrew" Hensel.

Catherine Workman was buried in 1877 in Calvary United Methodist, Wiconisco, Dauphin County, Pennsylvania, USA[62]. She was counted in the census in 1840 in Wiconisco, Dauphin County, Pennsylvania, USA ((unlisted)[137]). She was counted in the census in 1850 in Wiconisco, Dauphin County, Pennsylvania, USA[138]. She was counted in the census in 1860 in Porter, Schuylkill County, Pennsylvania, USA. She was counted in the census in 1870 in Wiconisco, Dauphin County, Pennsylvania, USA. She was employed as a Keeping house in 1870[71]. Her estate was probated on May 24, 1878.

Catherine Workman and Andrew Guise Hensel had the following children:

i.   John Henry William Hensel (son of Andrew Guise Hensel and Catherine Workman) was born in 1853 in Pennsylvania, USA. He died about Abt. 1854.

ii. Joseph Franklin Hensel (son of Andrew Guise Hensel and Catherine Workman) was born in 1854 in Pennsylvania, USA. He died in 1909. He married Agnes A Faust. She was born in 1855 in Pennsylvania, USA. She died in 1932.

iii. Ira Sylvester Hensel (son of Andrew Guise Hensel and Catherine Workman) was born in 1856 in Pennsylvania, USA. He died in 1916. He married Sarah Elizabeth Day. She was born in 1859 in Pennsylvania, USA. She died in 1922.

6.   iv. Howard Andrew Carson Hensel (son of Andrew Guise Hensel and Catherine Workman) was born on September 02, 1858 in Wiconisco, Dauphin County, Pennsylvania, USA[62, 63, 64]. He died on June 06, 1927 in Tower City, Schuylkill County, Pennsylvania, USA[62, 63, 64, 65]. He married Clara Matilda Updegrove (daughter of Daniel Updegrove and Sarah "Salome" A Culp) on September 02, 1884 in Wiconisco, Dauphin County, Pennsylvania, USA[62, 64]. She was born on November 30, 1866 in Lower Ranch Creek, Tremont, Schuylkill County, Pennsylvania, USA[62, 64]. She died on March 28, 1926 in Tower City, Schuylkill County, Pennsylvania, USA[62, 64, 66].

v.   Anna Catherine Hensel (daughter of Andrew Guise Hensel and Catherine Workman) was born about Abt. 1862 in Pennsylvania, USA.

vi. Lillian "Lillie" Emma Susan Hensel (daughter of Andrew Guise Hensel and Catherine Workman) was born in 1864 in Pennsylvania, USA. She married David Alfred Boyer. He was born in 1860. He died in 1940.

vii. Anne "Annie" Clarissa Workman Hensel (daughter of Andrew Guise Hensel and Catherine Workman) was born in 1866 in Pennsylvania, USA. She married Edward Beedle. He was born in 1863 in Pennsylvania, USA.

viii. Emma Hensel (daughter of Andrew Guise Hensel and Catherine Workman) was born in 1866 in Pennsylvania, USA.

14. **Daniel Updegrove** (son of John M Updegrove and Elizabeth Reisch) was born on June 28, 1839 in Wiconisco, Dauphin County, Pennsylvania, USA[139, 140]. He died on May 23, 1899 in Williamstown, Dauphin County, Pennsylvania, USA[141]. He married **Sarah "Salome" A Culp** (daughter of Jacob Kulp and Elizabeth Schneck) on October 09, 1862 in Dauphin County, Pennsylvania, USA.

15. **Sarah "Salome" A Culp** (daughter of Jacob Kulp and Elizabeth Schneck) was born on June 30, 1844 in Union County, Pennsylvania, USA[142]. She died on July 03, 1923 in Williamstown, Dauphin County, Pennsylvania, USA[142].

Daniel Updegrove was buried on May 28, 1899 in Seyberts (Old) Lutheran, Williamstown, Dauphin County, Pennsylvania, USA[139, 143]. His cause of death was Suffocated by mine gas[139]. He was counted in the census in 1840 in Wiconisco, Dauphin County, Pennsylvania, USA (w/father). He was counted in the census in 1850 in Wiconisco, Dauphin County, Pennsylvania, USA[144, 145]. He was counted in the census in 1860 in Brady, Lycoming County, Pennsylvania, USA ((Hullsizer)[146]). He was counted in the census in 1870 in Williamstown, Dauphin County, Pennsylvania, USA[79, 140, 147]. He was counted in the census in 1880 in Williamstown, Dauphin County, Pennsylvania, USA[80]. He was educated at School in 1850[148]. His height was 5 ft. 5 in.. He had a medical condition of Hair sandy, Complexion Light, Eyes grey, Daniel Updegrove, Civil War Veterans Card File, 1861-1866, Pennsylvania, USA, State Archives, www.digitalarchives.state.pa.us. He served in the military about Abt. 1863 in POW, 21 days, Libby Prison, Richmond, VA[149]. He served in the military on July 01, 1863 (Civil War, Private). He served in the military on August 16, 1864 (Civil War, Private, 9th Reg Pennsylvania,

USA Cav, Co B, 92nd Volunteers (Harrisburg, Capt. Edward Savage)[143, 150, 151, 152, 153]). He served in the military on May 16, 1889 in Pension App[154]. He was employed as a Blksmith App. in 1860[146]. He was employed as a Miner between 1864-1865[155]. He was employed as a Laborer in mine in 1870[79]. He was employed as a Laborer in 1880[80]. He was employed as a Miner (Brookside Colliery) in 1899[139]. He lived in Dauphin County, Pennsylvania, USA between 1864-1865[155]. He lived in Tower City, Schuylkill County, Pennsylvania, USA in 1890[152].

Sarah "Salome" A Culp was buried on July 06, 1923 in Seyberts (Old) Lutheran, Williamstown, Dauphin County, Pennsylvania, USA[142]. Her cause of death was ? due to carcinoma of shoulder (recurrent) w/secondary ?[142]. She was counted in the census in 1850 in West Buffalo, Union County, Pennsylvania, USA[156]. She was counted in the census in 1860 in Buffalo, Union County, Pennsylvania, USA[157]. She was counted in the census in 1870 in Williamstown, Dauphin County, Pennsylvania, USA[79]. She was counted in the census in 1880 in Williamstown, Dauphin County, Pennsylvania, USA. She was counted in the census in 1900[158]. She was counted in the census in 1910 in Williamstown, Dauphin County, Pennsylvania, USA ((Shadel)[159]). She was counted in the census in 1920 in Tower City, Schuylkill County, Pennsylvania, USA ((Weist)[160]). She was educated at School in 1850[161]. She was employed as a Keeping house between 1870-1880[79, 80]. She was employed as a Domestic in 1923[142]. Her estate was probated between April 02-08 1927 in Harrisburg, Dauphin County, Pennsylvania, USA[162]. She lived in Pottsville St., Williams, Dauphin County, Pennsylvania, USA in 1910[159]. She lived in 25 West Grand Ave., Tower City, Schuylkill County, Pennsylvania, USA in 1920[160]. Funeral: 1923 in Aaron Ralphsson, Williamstown, Dauphin County, Pennsylvania, USA[142] Pension: May 1899 in Pennsylvania, USA[163]

Notes for Sarah "Salome" A Culp:
Maiden name listed as Hoffman [Updegrove family information, Updegrove Genealogy, PA State library]

Sarah "Salome" A Culp and Daniel Updegrove had the following children:

    i.   Anna Minerva Updegrove (daughter of Daniel Updegrove and Sarah "Salome" A Culp) was born in 1864 in Pennsylvania, USA. She died in 1921. She married ? Schoffstall.

7.   ii.   Clara Matilda Updegrove (daughter of Daniel Updegrove and Sarah "Salome" A Culp) was born on November 30, 1866 in Lower Ranch Creek, Tremont, Schuylkill County, Pennsylvania, USA[62, 64]. She died on March 28, 1926 in Tower City, Schuylkill County, Pennsylvania, USA[62, 64, 66]. She married Howard Andrew Carson Hensel (son of Andrew Guise Hensel and Catherine Workman) on September 02, 1884 in Wiconisco, Dauphin County, Pennsylvania, USA[62, 64]. He was born on September 02, 1858 in Wiconisco, Dauphin County, Pennsylvania, USA[62, 63, 64]. He died on June 06, 1927 in Tower City, Schuylkill County, Pennsylvania, USA[62, 63, 64, 65].

    iii.   William Henry Updegrove (son of Daniel Updegrove and Sarah "Salome" A Culp) was born in 1870 in Pennsylvania, USA. He died in 1871. He married Catherine "Kate" ?.

    iv.   Nora Jane Updegrove (daughter of Daniel Updegrove and Sarah "Salome" A Culp) was born in 1874 in Pennsylvania, USA. She married Henry L Shadel. He was born in 1865 in Pennsylvania, USA.

Generation 5

16. **Robert Thompson** (son of Robert Thomson and Mary Black) was born on June 27, 1771 in Edgehead, Cranston, Midlothian, Scotland[82]. He died about Abt. 1852 in Edgehead, Midlothian, Scotland[164]. He married **Janet Russell** (daughter of William Russell and Christina Moffatt) on April 22, 1791 in Borthwick, Newbattle, Midlothian, Scotland[48, 61, 82, 165].

17. **Janet Russell** (daughter of William Russell and Christina Moffatt) was born on December 21, 1766 in Newbattle, Midlothian, Scotland[48, 82]. She died after Aft. 1811 in Midlothian, Scotland[164].

Robert Thompson was born in 1766 in Borthwick, Midlothian, Scotland[166]. He was employed as a Coalier (Earl of Stair) about Abt. 1810[82]. He was employed as a Coal Overseer[83].

Janet Russell and Robert Thompson had the following children:

i. Christina Thompson (daughter of Robert Thompson and Janet Russell) was born in 1792 in Scotland. She married John King.

ii. Robert Thompson (son of Robert Thompson and Janet Russell) was born in 1795 in Scotland. He married Elizabeth Wilson.

iii. William Thompson (son of Robert Thompson and Janet Russell) was born in 1797 in Scotland. He married Anna Penman.

iv. Mary Thompson (daughter of Robert Thompson and Janet Russell) was born in 1800 in Scotland. She married James Wilson.

v. George W Thompson (son of Robert Thompson and Janet Russell) was born in 1802 in Scotland. He married Catherine Penman. She was born on July 12, 1802 in Newbattle, Midlothian, Scotland. He married Margaret McLeran. She was born in 1816.

vi. John Thompson (son of Robert Thompson and Janet Russell) was born in 1804 in Scotland.

8.   vii. Alexander Thompson (son of Robert Thompson and Janet Russell) was born on October 22, 1805 in Sauchenside Farm, Cranston, Midlothian, Scotland[82, 83, 84, 85]. He died on December 04, 1873 in Tower City, Schuylkill County, Pennsylvania, USA[61, 86, 87]. He married Isabelle Stoddart Penman (daughter of David Penman and Elizabeth Stoddart) on January 01, 1835 in Pottsville, Schuylkill County, Pennsylvania, USA[82]. She was born on May 09, 1816 in Newbattle, Midlothian, Scotland[61]. She died on April 18, 1851 in Pottsville, Schuylkill County, Pennsylvania, USA[88]. He married Mary A Bast in 1853.

She was born in 1833 in Pennsylvania, USA. She died in 1910.

    viii. John Thompson (son of Robert Thompson and Janet Russell) was born in 1808 in Scotland.

    ix. James Smith Thompson (son of Robert Thompson and Janet Russell) was born in 1811 in Scotland.

18. **David Penman** (son of John Penman and Catherine Brown) was born on December 31, 1775 in Newbattle, Midlothian, Scotland[100, 167]. He died in 1825 in Newbattle, Midlothian, Scotland[100]. He married **Elizabeth Stoddart** (daughter of David Stoddart and Margaret Muckle) about Abt. 1800 in Scotland.

19. **Elizabeth Stoddart** (daughter of David Stoddart and Margaret Muckle) was born on January 05, 1779 in Stobgreen Temple, Edinburgh, Midlothian, Scotland[100, 167]. She died on December 25, 1849 in Pottsville, Schuylkill County, Pennsylvania, USA[100, 167].

David Penman was born on December 14, 1775[168].

Notes for David Penman:
s/o John Penman

Elizabeth Stoddart was buried in 1849 in Presbyterian Burial Grounds, Pottsville, Schuylkill County, Pennsylvania, USA[169]. She was counted in the census in 1830. She was counted in the census in 1840 in Norwegian, Schuylkill County, Pennsylvania, USA[170]. She was counted in the census in 1841 in Liberton, Midlothian, Scotland[171]. She immigrated before Bef. 1830. She was employed as a Pauper sup by children in 1841[171].

Elizabeth Stoddart and David Penman had the following children:
    i. Miriam Penman (daughter of David Penman and Elizabeth Stoddart) was born in Scotland.

    ii. John Penman (son of David Penman and Elizabeth

Stoddart) was born on April 18, 1798 in Newbattle, Midlothian, Scotland[172].

iii. Margaret Penman (daughter of David Penman and Elizabeth Stoddart) was born on July 20, 1800 in Newbattle, Midlothian, Scotland.

iv. Catherine Penman (daughter of David Penman and Elizabeth Stoddart) was born on July 12, 1802 in Newbattle, Midlothian, Scotland. She married George W Thompson. He was born in 1802 in Scotland.

v. Elizabeth Penman (daughter of David Penman and Elizabeth Stoddart) was born on February 22, 1807 in Newbattle, Midlothian, Scotland.

vi. Anne Penman (daughter of David Penman and Elizabeth Stoddart) was born on June 13, 1809 in Inveresk, Midlothian, Scotland.

vii. James Penman (son of David Penman and Elizabeth Stoddart) was born on October 12, 1811 in Newbattle, Midlothian, Scotland.

9. viii. Isabelle Stoddart Penman (daughter of David Penman and Elizabeth Stoddart) was born on May 09, 1816 in Newbattle, Midlothian, Scotland[61]. She died on April 18, 1851 in Pottsville, Schuylkill County, Pennsylvania, USA[88]. She married Alexander Thompson (son of Robert Thompson and Janet Russell) on January 01, 1835 in Pottsville, Schuylkill County, Pennsylvania, USA[82]. He was born on October 22, 1805 in Sauchenside Farm, Cranston, Midlothian, Scotland[82, 83, 84, 85]. He died on December 04, 1873 in Tower City, Schuylkill County, Pennsylvania, USA[61, 86, 87].

ix. Alexander Penman (son of David Penman and Elizabeth Stoddart) was born on October 24, 1820 in Newbattle, Midlothian, Scotland.

x. Robert Penman (son of David Penman and Elizabeth

Stoddart) was born on December 11, 1824 in Newbattle, Midlothian, Scotland.

20. **John George Gutman** (son of Wilhelm Guthman and Elizabeth ?) was born on January 18, 1776 in Pennsylvania, USA[173]. He died about Abt. 1810 in Pennsylvania, USA[102, 174]. He married **? Brown** (daughter of Peter Braun and Catherine ?) about Abt. 1800 in Pennsylvania, USA.

21. **? Brown** (daughter of Peter Braun and Catherine ?) was born about Abt. 1782 in Berks (Schuylkill) County, Pennsylvania, USA. She died after Aft. 1810.

    ? Brown and John George Gutman had the following children:

    i.   Benjamin Goodman (son of John George Gutman and ? Brown) was born about Abt. 1801 in Pennsylvania, USA. He died between 1880-1900. He married Elizabeth ?.

    ii. Daniel Gutman (son of John George Gutman and ? Brown) was born in 1803 in Pennsylvania, USA. He died between 1880-1900. He married Catherine ?.

    10. iii. Michael Goodman (son of John George Gutman and ? Brown) was born on June 10, 1806 in Lower Mahanoy Northumberland County, Pennsylvania, USA[101, 102, 103]. He died on December 27, 1900 in Rush, Dauphin County, Pennsylvania, USA[101, 104]. He married Mary Magdalena Brown (daughter of Peter Braun Brown and Anna Maria ?) about Abt. 1849 in Schuylkill County, Pennsylvania, USA. She was born in 1816 in Rush, Dauphin Co., ,Pennsylvania. She died on December 17, 1884 in Tower City, Schuylkill, Pennsylvania[101]. He married Mary Barbara Ramp about Abt. 1830. She was born about Abt. 1805 in Pennsylvania, USA.

22. **Peter Braun Brown** (son of Peter Braun and Catherine ?) was born about Abt. 1780 in Berks (Schuylkill) County, Pennsylvania, USA. He died about Abt. 1859 in Rush Township, Dauphin County, Pennsylvania, USA[175]. He married **Anna Maria ?** (daughter of ? and ?) about Abt. 1812 in Dauphin County, Pennsylvania, USA.

23. **Anna Maria ?** (daughter of ? and ?) was born about Abt. 1797 in Dauphin Co., ,Pennsylvania[176]. She died on April 10, 1879 in Rush, Dauphin County, Pennsylvania, USA[176].

Peter Braun Brown was counted in the census in 1790[177]. He was counted in the census in 1800[178]. He was counted in the census in 1810 in Lower Mahantango, Berks County, Pennsylvania, USA (w/father[179]). He was counted in the census in 1820 in Rush, Dauphin County, Pennsylvania, USA[180]. He was counted in the census in 1830 in Rush, Dauphin County, Pennsylvania, USA[181]. He was counted in the census in 1840 in Rush, Dauphin County, Pennsylvania, USA[182]. He was counted in the census in 1850 in Rush, Dauphin County, Pennsylvania, USA[183, 184]. He was counted in the census in 1860. He was employed as a Laborer about Abt. 1835. He was employed as a Weaver in 1850[183]. He lived in Clarks Valley, Pennsylvania, USA, now Charles Kessler farm in 1916[185].

Anna Maria ? was buried on April 13, 1879 in McCallister's Methodist Cemetery, Rush, Dauphin County, Pennsylvania, USA[186]. She was counted in the census in 1800. She was counted in the census in 1810. She was counted in the census in 1820 in Rush, Dauphin County, Pennsylvania, USA (w/husband). She was counted in the census in 1830 in Rush, Dauphin County, Pennsylvania, USA (w/husband). She was counted in the census in 1840 in Rush, Dauphin County, Pennsylvania, USA (w/husband). She was counted in the census in 1850 in Rush, Dauphin County, Pennsylvania, USA. She was counted in the census in 1860 in Rush, Dauphin County, Pennsylvania, USA (w/son John Brown[187]). She was counted in the census in 1870. She immigrated before Bef. 1820.

Notes for Anna Maria ?:
Also listed born Germany

Anna Maria ? and Peter Braun Brown had the following children:
  i.   John Brown (son of Peter Braun Brown and Anna Maria ?) was born in 1812 in Pennsylvania, USA. He married Catherine Hautz?.

ii. Peter Brown (son of Peter Braun Brown and Anna Maria ?) was born in 1814 in Pennsylvania, USA. He married Anna Maria ?. She was born in 1810 in Pennsylvania, USA.

iii. Anna Maria Brown (daughter of Peter Braun Brown and Anna Maria ?) was born on February 17, 1815 in Clarks Valley, Dauphin County, Pennsylvania, USA[176]. She died on September 07, 1891 in Dauphin, Pennsylvania, USA[176]. She married William Miller. He was born in 1813 in Pennsylvania, USA.

11. iv. Mary Magdalena Brown (daughter of Peter Braun Brown and Anna Maria ?) was born in 1816 in Rush, Dauphin Co., ,Pennsylvania. She died on December 17, 1884 in Tower City, Schuylkill, Pennsylvania[101]. She married Michael Goodman (son of John George Gutman and ? Brown) about Abt. 1849 in Schuylkill County, Pennsylvania, USA. He was born on June 10, 1806 in Lower Mahanoy Northumberland County, Pennsylvania, USA[101, 102, 103]. He died on December 27, 1900 in Rush, Dauphin County, Pennsylvania, USA[101, 104].

v. William Brown (son of Peter Braun Brown and Anna Maria ?) was born in 1818 in Pennsylvania, USA. He married Ellen Updegrove. She was born about Abt. 1812 in Pennsylvania, USA.

vi. Philip Brown (son of Peter Braun Brown and Anna Maria ?) was born in 1821 in Pennsylvania, USA.

vii. Rebecca Brown (daughter of Peter Braun Brown and Anna Maria ?) was born about Abt. 1825 in Pennsylvania, USA.

viii. Elizabeth Brown (daughter of Peter Braun Brown and Anna Maria ?) was born in 1830 in Pennsylvania, USA.

24. **Andrew W Hensel** (son of John Casper Hensel and Anna Maria Eva ?) was born on June 28, 1793 in Littlestown, York (Adams) County, Pennsylvania, USA[188, 189]. He died on July 07, 1875 in Home, New Bloomfield, Perry County, Pennsylvania, USA[190, 191]. He married **Mary A Guise** (daughter of John Adam Guise and Maria? ?) about Abt.

1814 in Adams, Pennsylvania, USA[120].

25. **Mary A Guise** (daughter of John Adam Guise and Maria? ?) was born on December 16, 1791 in Northampton County, Pennsylvania, USA. She died on January 16, 1877 in New Bloomfield, Perry County, Pennsylvania, USA[192, 193, 194].

Andrew W Hensel was baptized on August 11, 1793 in Christ Reformed, Littlestown, York (Adams) County, Pennsylvania, USA[188, 189]. He was buried in July 1875 in St. Peters (Christ, Old Union) Cemetery, New Bloomfield, Perry County, Pennsylvania, USA[120, 195]. He was counted in the census in 1800 in Maheim, York County, Pennsylvania, USA (w/father[196]). He was counted in the census in 1810. He was counted in the census in 1820 in Mount Joy, Adams County, Pennsylvania, USA ((Hensle)[197]). He was counted in the census in 1830 in Juniata, Perry County, Pennsylvania, USA[198]. He was counted in the census in 1840 in Centre, Perry County, Pennsylvania, USA ((Hensley)[199]). He was counted in the census in 1850 in Centre, Perry County, Pennsylvania, USA[124]. He was counted in the census in 1860 in Centre, Perry County, Pennsylvania, USA ((Miller)[200]). He was counted in the census in 1870 in Centre, Perry County, Pennsylvania, USA ((Hentzelle)[201]). He served in the military in February 1814 (War of 1812, Private, 5th Reg Pennsylvania, USA Militia (Fentons), detachment (Adams, Capt. John McMillan)[120, 190, 202]). He was employed as a Laborer in 1850[124]. He was employed as a Deacon (Christ's Church, Bloomfield, Perry County, Pennsylvania, USA) between 1850-1855[203]. He was employed as a Farmer in 1860[200]. He was employed as a Hostler about Abt. 1865. He was employed as a Laborer in 1870[201]. His estate was probated on August 13, 1875 in Perry County, Pennsylvania, USA[204]. His estate was probated on May 24, 1878 in Dauphin County, Pennsylvania, USA[205]. He was affiliated with the Lutheran & German Reformed Church religion in 1875[120, 190]. He lived in near Gettysburg, Adams County, Pennsylvania, USA in 1823[206]. He signed his will between March-December 1864 in Centre, Perry County, Pennsylvania, USA[204]. Political Party: in Democrat[207]

Mary A Guise was buried in January 1877 in St. Peters (Christ, Old

Union) Cemetery, New Bloomfield, Perry County, Pennsylvania, USA[120, 208]. She was counted in the census in 1800[209]. She was counted in the census in 1810[210]. She was counted in the census in 1820 in Mount Joy, Adams County, Pennsylvania, USA (w/husband[211]). She was counted in the census in 1830 in Juniata, Perry County, Pennsylvania, USA (w/husband). She was counted in the census in 1840 in Centre, Perry County, Pennsylvania, USA (w/husband). She was counted in the census in 1850 in Centre, Perry County, Pennsylvania, USA. She was counted in the census in 1860 in Centre, Perry County, Pennsylvania, USA. She was counted in the census in 1870 in Centre, Perry County, Pennsylvania, USA. She was employed as a Invalid in 1870[201].

Mary A Guise and Andrew W Hensel had the following children:

i.   John Adam Hensel (son of Andrew W Hensel and Mary A Guise) was born in 1814 in Pennsylvania, USA. He married Anna Maria Haverstick.

ii. Anna Maria Barbara Hensel (daughter of Andrew W Hensel and Mary A Guise) was born in 1820 in Pennsylvania, USA. She died about Abt. 1890. She married David Swartz. He was born in 1816 in Pennsylvania, USA.

iii. John Hensel (son of Andrew W Hensel and Mary A Guise) was born in 1824 in Perry County, Pennsylvania, USA. He died in Lykens, Dauphin County, Pennsylvania, USA. He married Susan Moyer. She was born in 1833 in Pennsylvania, USA.

iv. George Hensel (son of Andrew W Hensel and Mary A Guise) was born in 1825 in Perry County, Pennsylvania, USA. He died in IL.

12. v. Andrew Guise Hensel (son of Andrew W Hensel and Mary A Guise) was born on February 18, 1831 in Home, New Bloomfield, Perry County, Pennsylvania, USA[62, 118, 119, 120]. He died on December 14, 1908 in Wiconisco, Dauphin County, Pennsylvania, USA[62, 121]. He married Catherine Workman (daughter of Joseph Workman and Susan Romberger) on May 17, 1853 in Halifax, Dauphin County,

Pennsylvania, USA[118, 119]. She was born on May 17, 1838 in Old Lincoln, Dauphin County, Pennsylvania, USA[62]. She died on February 10, 1877 in Joliett, Schuylkill County, Pennsylvania, USA[62]. He married Grace Arrison about Abt. 1878. She was born in 1823. She died in 1893[81].

    vi.   Michael Hensel (son of Andrew W Hensel and Mary A Guise) was born in 1834 in Perry County, Pennsylvania, USA. He died in 1915. He married Elizabeth ?. She was born in 1837 in Pennsylvania, USA.

Notes for Michael Hensel:
Reverend

26. **Joseph Workman** (son of Benjamin? Workman and Priscilla Doss?) was born on December 03, 1795 in Lykens, Dauphin County, Pennsylvania, USA[62, 212]. He died on May 23, 1857 in Wiconisco, Dauphin County, Pennsylvania, USA[62, 212, 213, 214]. He married **Susan Romberger** (daughter of Balthasar Romberger and Susan Lehman) about Abt. 1818 in Dauphin County, Pennsylvania, USA[215].

27. **Susan Romberger** (daughter of Balthasar Romberger and Susan Lehman) was born on April 16, 1799 in Lykens, Dauphin County, Pennsylvania, USA[62, 212, 216, 217]. She died on February 23, 1857 in Wiconisco, Dauphin County, Pennsylvania, USA[62, 215, 216].

Joseph Workman was buried in 1857 in Calvary United Methodist, Wiconisco, Dauphin County, Pennsylvania, USA[62, 212, 213]. He was counted in the census in 1800. He was counted in the census in 1810. He was counted in the census in 1820 in Lykens, Dauphin County, Pennsylvania, USA[218]. He was counted in the census in 1830 in Lykens, Dauphin County, Pennsylvania, USA ((James)[219]). He was counted in the census in 1840 in Wiconisco, Dauphin County, Pennsylvania, USA[137]. He was counted in the census in 1850 in Wiconisco, Dauphin County, Pennsylvania, USA[138, 220]. He was confirmed in 1827 in Zion Union, Tower City, Schuylkill County, Pennsylvania, USA. He served in the military between September 01, 1814-March 05, 1825 (War of 1812, Private, 2nd Reg Pennsylvania, USA Militia (Ritschers), 1st Brig (York, Capt. Jacob District)). He was employed as a Agriculture in 1820[218]. He was employed as a Farmer in 1850[138]. He was employed as a School director about Abt. 1850. His estate was probated on June 18, 1857 in Dauphin County, Pennsylvania, USA(listed in index only)[221]. He was affiliated with the St. Johns (Hill) Lutheran, Lykens, Dauphin County, Pennsylvania, USA religion in 1819[222].

Susan Romberger was baptized on April 16, 1799[223]. She was baptized on July 07, 1799 in St. Johns (Hill) Lutheran, Berrysburg, Dauphin County, Pennsylvania, USA[67]. She was buried in 1857 in Calvary United Methodist, Wiconisco, Dauphin County, Pennsylvania, USA[62]. She was counted in the census in 1800 in Upper Paxton, Dauphin County, Pennsylvania, USA (w/father[224]). She was counted in the census in 1810 in Upper Paxton, Dauphin County, Pennsylvania, USA (w/father[225]). She was counted in the census in 1820 in Lykens, Dauphin County, Pennsylvania, USA (w/husband). She was counted in the census in 1830. She was counted in the census in 1840 in Wiconisco, Dauphin County, Pennsylvania, USA (w/husband). She was counted in the census in 1850 in Wiconisco, Dauphin County, Pennsylvania, USA. She was confirmed in 1827 in Zion Union, Tower City, Schuylkill County, Pennsylvania, USA. She was affiliated with the Upper Paxton, Dauphin County, Pennsylvania, USA[216] religion.

Notes for Susan Romberger:
Maiden name listed as Myers [Hensel family information, Dauphin Co Marriages, 1852-1855, CAGS]

Susan Romberger and Joseph Workman had the following children:
    i.   Jacob Workman (son of Joseph Workman and Susan Romberger) was born in 1819 in Dauphin County, Pennsylvania, USA. He married Mary ?. She was born in 1826 in Pennsylvania, USA.

    ii.   Susan Workman (daughter of Joseph Workman and Susan Romberger) was born in 1821 in Dauphin County, Pennsylvania, USA. She married David S Doebler. He was born in 1816. He died in 1869. She married Louis A

Greshammer. He was born in 1835. He died in 1870.

iii. John Workman (son of Joseph Workman and Susan Romberger) was born in 1823 in Pennsylvania, USA. He died in 1858. He married Sidnam ?. She was born in 1824 in Pennsylvania, USA.

iv. Nancy Workman (daughter of Joseph Workman and Susan Romberger) was born in 1826 in Pennsylvania, USA. She married Emmanuel Sassaman. He was born in 1827 in Pennsylvania, USA. She married Henry Singer. He was born in 1825.

v. Elizabeth Workman (daughter of Joseph Workman and Susan Romberger) was born in 1829 in Dauphin County, Pennsylvania, USA. She married Isaac Smink. He was born in 1828 in Pennsylvania, USA.

vi. Carolina Workman (daughter of Joseph Workman and Susan Romberger) was born in 1831 in Pennsylvania, USA.

vii. Henry Workman (son of Joseph Workman and Susan Romberger) was born in 1833 in Pennsylvania, USA. He married Juliana ?. She was born in 1841 in Ireland (Pennsylvania, USA).

viii. Joseph R Workman (son of Joseph Workman and Susan Romberger) was born in 1836 in Pennsylvania, USA. He died in 1916. He married Susan ?. She was born in 1838 in Pennsylvania, USA. She died in 1899.

13. ix. Catherine Workman (daughter of Joseph Workman and Susan Romberger) was born on May 17, 1838 in Old Lincoln, Dauphin County, Pennsylvania, USA[62]. She died on February 10, 1877 in Joliett, Schuylkill County, Pennsylvania, USA[62]. She married Andrew Guise Hensel (son of Andrew W Hensel and Mary A Guise) on May 17, 1853 in Halifax, Dauphin County, Pennsylvania, USA[118, 119]. He was born on February 18, 1831 in Home, New Bloomfield, Perry County, Pennsylvania, USA[62, 118, 119, 120].

He died on December 14, 1908 in Wiconisco, Dauphin County, Pennsylvania, USA[62, 121].

28. **John M Updegrove** (son of Conrad Updegrove and Maria Elizabeth Angst) was born on March 23, 1805 in Berks County, Pennsylvania, USA[226, 227]. He died about Abt. 1864 in Clinton, Lycoming County, Pennsylvania, USA[227, 228]. He married **Elizabeth Reisch** (daughter of Frederick Reisch and Veronica Schmidt) about Abt. 1826 in Dauphin County, Pennsylvania, USA[229].

29. **Elizabeth Reisch** (daughter of Frederick Reisch and Veronica Schmidt) was born on January 15, 1802 in Dauphin County, Pennsylvania, USA[229, 230]. She died between 1860-1870 in Clinton, Lycoming County, Pennsylvania, USA[229].

John M Updegrove was baptized on April 14, 1805 in St. Jacobs Lutheran, Pine Grove, Berks (Schuylkill) County, Pennsylvania, USA[226]. He was counted in the census in 1810 in Jonestown, Dauphin (Lebanon) County, Pennsylvania, USA (w/father[231]). He was counted in the census in 1820 in Lykens, Dauphin County, Pennsylvania, USA (w/father[232]). He was counted in the census in 1830[233]. He was counted in the census in 1840 in Wiconisco, Dauphin County, Pennsylvania, USA[234]. He was counted in the census in 1850 in Wiconisco, Dauphin County, Pennsylvania, USA[145, 148]. He was counted in the census in 1860 in Clinton, Lycoming County, Pennsylvania, USA[235]. He was employed as a Labor in 1850[148]. He was employed as a Laborer in 1860[235].

Elizabeth Reisch was counted in the census in 1810. She was counted in the census in 1820. She was counted in the census in 1830. She was counted in the census in 1840 in Wiconisco, Dauphin County, Pennsylvania, USA (w/husband). She was counted in the census in 1850 in Wiconisco, Dauphin County, Pennsylvania, USA. She was counted in the census in 1860 in Clinton, Lycoming County, Pennsylvania, USA.

Notes for Elizabeth Reisch:
Possibly daughter of Trovinger, but may be confused with son John J

who married Eliz Trovinger.

Elizabeth Reisch and John M Updegrove had the following children:
  i.   Jacob Updegrove (son of John M Updegrove and Elizabeth Reisch) was born in 1827 in Pennsylvania, USA. He married Sophia ?. She was born in 1835 in Pennsylvania, USA.

  ii.   Catherine Updegrove (daughter of John M Updegrove and Elizabeth Reisch) was born in 1833 in Pennsylvania, USA.

  iii. John J Updegrove (son of John M Updegrove and Elizabeth Reisch) was born in 1835 in Pennsylvania, USA. He died in 1901. He married Elizabeth ?. She was born in 1839 in OH.

  iv.   Nancy Updegrove (daughter of John M Updegrove and Elizabeth Reisch) was born in 1838 in Pennsylvania, USA.

14. v.   Daniel Updegrove (son of John M Updegrove and Elizabeth Reisch) was born on June 28, 1839 in Wiconisco, Dauphin County, Pennsylvania, USA[139, 140]. He died on May 23, 1899 in Williamstown, Dauphin County, Pennsylvania, USA[141]. He married Sarah "Salome" A Culp (daughter of Jacob Kulp and Elizabeth Schneck) on October 09, 1862 in Dauphin County, Pennsylvania, USA. She was born on June 30, 1844 in Union County, Pennsylvania, USA[142]. She died on July 03, 1923 in Williamstown, Dauphin County, Pennsylvania, USA[142].

  vi.   Solomon Updegrove (son of John M Updegrove and Elizabeth Reisch) was born in 1845 in Pennsylvania, USA. He died in 1864.

  vii. Rebecca Updegrove (daughter of John M Updegrove and Elizabeth Reisch) was born in 1847 in Pennsylvania, USA.

30. **Jacob Kulp** (son of ? Kulp and ?) was born about Abt. 1802 in Pennsylvania, USA. He died about Abt. 1865 in Union County, Pennsylvania, USA. He married **Elizabeth Schneck** (daughter of Peter Schneck and Mary ?) about Abt. 1835 in Union County,

Pennsylvania, USA.

31. **Elizabeth Schneck** (daughter of Peter Schneck and Mary ?) was born on August 13, 1805 in Northumberland (Union) County, Pennsylvania, USA[236]. She died on June 02, 1861 in Mifflinburg, Union, Pennsylvania, USA[236, 237].

Jacob Kulp was counted in the census in 1810. He was counted in the census in 1820. He was counted in the census in 1830. He was counted in the census in 1840. He was counted in the census in 1850 in West Buffalo, Union County, Pennsylvania, USA[156, 236, 238]. He was counted in the census in 1860 in Buffalo, Union County, Pennsylvania, USA[157]. He was employed as a Carpenter in 1850[156, 238]. He was employed as a Laborer in 1860[239].

Elizabeth Schneck was buried in 1861 in St John´s United Church of Christ, Mifflinburg Cemetery, Union County, Pennsylvania, USA[237, 240]. Her cause of death was Diseased liver[237]. She was counted in the census in 1810 in Centre, Northumberland (Union) County, Pennsylvania, USA (w/father[241]). She was counted in the census in 1820[242]. She was counted in the census in 1830. She was counted in the census in 1840. She was counted in the census in 1850 in West Buffalo, Union County, Pennsylvania, USA. She was counted in the census in 1860 in Buffalo, Union County, Pennsylvania, USA. She was employed as a Homemaker about Abt. 1840.

Elizabeth Schneck and Jacob Kulp had the following children:
  i. Jonas Culp (son of Jacob Kulp and Elizabeth Schneck) was born in 1839 in Pennsylvania, USA.

  ii. Elizabeth Culp (daughter of Jacob Kulp and Elizabeth Schneck) was born in 1842 in Pennsylvania, USA.

  iii. Henrietta Culp (daughter of Jacob Kulp and Elizabeth Schneck) was born in 1842 in Pennsylvania, USA.

  iv. Esther Culp (daughter of Jacob Kulp and Elizabeth Schneck) was born in 1844 in Pennsylvania, USA.

15. v.   Sarah "Salome" A Culp (daughter of Jacob Kulp and
          Elizabeth Schneck) was born on June 30, 1844 in Union
          County, Pennsylvania, USA[142]. She died on July 03, 1923
          in Williamstown, Dauphin County, Pennsylvania, USA[142].
          She married Daniel Updegrove (son of John M Updegrove
          and Elizabeth Reisch) on October 09, 1862 in Dauphin
          County, Pennsylvania, USA. He was born on June 28,
          1839 in Wiconisco, Dauphin County, Pennsylvania,
          USA[139, 140]. He died on May 23, 1899 in Williamstown,
          Dauphin County, Pennsylvania, USA[141].

    vi.   Fielta Culp (daughter of Jacob Kulp and Elizabeth
          Schneck) was born in 1848 in Pennsylvania, USA.

Sources

1 Harper Bruce Thompson birth record, #344701, #122649-07,
  September 1907, Schuylkill Co, PA, Department of Vital Records,
  New Castle, PA.
2 Harper B Thompson death certificate, #2501265, Department of
  Vital Records, New Castle, PA.
3 Harper B Thompson, Obituary, Harrisburg Patriot Newspaper, July
  1981.
4 Thompson-Batdorf marriage record, Register of Wills, Clerk of
  Orphans Court, Dauphin Co, PA, 1935.
5 Samuel Peters, Descendants of John Peters, Evelyn S. Hartman.
6 Myrtle A. Batdorf birth certificate, January 1918, Department of
  Vital records, New Castle, PA.
7 Myrtle Thompson, Obituary, Harrisburg Patriot newspaper, 1983.
8 Myrtle A Thompson death certificate, #3455802, Department of
  Vital records, New Castle, PA.
9 Thompson household, 1910 United States Census, Schuylkill Co,
  PA, www.ancestry.com and 1910 United States Census, Schuylkill
  Co, PA, ED 62, Sheet 32A, PA State Library.
10 Thompson household, 1920 United States Census, Schuylkill Co,
   PA, Roll T625 1651, ED 84, Image 0280, ancestry.com &
   Microfilm, PA State Library, Hbg, PA.
11 Thompson household, 1920 United States Census, Schuylkill Co,
   PA, PA State library, microfilm image.
12 Knittle household, 1930 United States Census, Lehigh Co, PA,
   ancestry.com & Microfilm, PA State Library, Hbg, PA.

13 Thompson household, US Federal Census 1940, Schuylkill, PA, SD 13, ED 54172, Sh 7A, ancestry.com.

14 Thompson household, 1920 United States Census, Schuylkill Co, PA, Roll T625 1651, ED 84, Image 0280, www.ancestry.com and 1920 United States Census, Schuylkill Co, PA, PA State library, microfilm image.

15 Harper B Thompson, Social Security numident record, application for SS-5, SSA, Nov 2006, Baltimore, MD.

16 Harper Thompson, July 1981, PA, Social Security Death Index, www.familysearch,org.

17 Batdorf household, 1920 United States Census, Dauphin Co, PA, Roll T625 1559, p 3A, ED 148, Image 1081, ancestry.com & Microfilm, PA State Library, Hbg, PA.

18 Batdorf household, 1930 United States Census, Dauphin Co, PA, Roll T626 2027, p 19A, ED 76, Image 0959, ancestry.com & Microfilm, PA State Library, Hbg, PA.

19 Batdorf household, 1930 United States Census, Dauphin Co, PA, Roll T626 2027, p 19A, ED 76, Image 0959, ancestry.com & Microfilm, PA State Library, Hbg, PA.

20 Myrtle A Thompson, Probate files, 1983, File 424-1983, Dauphin County Courthouse, Reg of Wills, Deborah Hershey, Elizabethtown, PA, Mar 2008.

21 Myrtle Thompson, Gerald G Thompson.

22 Myrtle Thompson, May 1983, PA, Social Security Death Index, www.familysearch.org.

23 Myrtle A Thompson, Obituary, Harrisburg Patriot newspaper, 1983.

24 Abel Thompson death certificate, #0506211, #133775-93, January 1918, Department of Vital Records, New castle, PC.

25 Thompson-Hensel Marriage, Office of the Register of Wills, Schuylkill County, PA, June 1904.

26 Abel Robert Thompson, WW I Draft Reg Cards, 1917-1918 Record, www.ancestry.com.

27 Abel R Thompson, Probate file, 1918, unnumbered original papers, 34pp, Schuylkill Co Courthouse, Schuylkill, PA, Norman Nicol, Apr 2008.

28 Gussie May Thompson death certificate, #0506187, #31982, March 1973, Department of Vital Records, New Castle, PA.

29 Gussie May Hensel, Funeral obituary, March 1973.

30 Gussie Mae Thompson, Obituary, Pottsville Repulbican, Pottsville, PA, March 28, 1973.

31 Gussie M. Thompson, Greenwood Cemetery, Tower City, Schuylkill Co, PA, John Barket, Tower City, PA, B-3-1.

32 Gussie M. Thompson, Reg of Will book, Book 145, pp578-82, May 27, 1950, probated Sept 11, 1973, Schuylkill Co Courthouse, Schuylkill, PA, Norman Nicol, Apr 2008.

33 Abel Thompson, Greenwood Cemetery, Tower City, Schuylkill Co, PA, John Barket, Tower City, PA, B-3-1.

34 Thompson household, 1900 United States Census, Schuylkill Co, PA www.ancestry.com, Liz McKinnon.

35 Abel R Thompson, 1918, Schuylkill County Register of Wills, Schuylkill Co, PA, #284.

36 Hensel household, 1900 United States Census, Schuylkill Co, PA, ww.ancestry.com and 1900 United States Census, Schuylkill Co, PA, PA State library microfilm image.

37 Thompson household, 1930 United States Census, Schuylkill Co, PA, Roll T626 2146, p 3A, ED 84, Image 0462, ancestry.com & Microfilm, PA State Library, Hbg, PA.

38 Thompson household, US Federal Census 1940, Schuylkill, PA, SD 13, ED 54-102, Sh 2B, ancestry.com.

39 Gussie Thompson, March 1973, PA, Social Security Death Index, www.familysearch.org.

40 Gussie May Thompson, #0506187, #31982, March 1973, Department of Vital Records, New Castle, PA.

41 Gussie May Thompson, Funeral obituary, March 1973.

42 Gussie M. Thompson, Obituary, Pottsville Republican, Pottsville, PA, March 28, 1973.

43 Michael Goodman, Descendants of Michael Goodman, Evelyn S Hartman, deanh@voicenet.com.

44 Abel F Thompson, Bob Averell Family Tree, Entries: 7956, Updated: 2004-08-01 00:29:03 UTC (Sun), Contact: Bob Averell.

45 Lydia Mae Thompson, Obituary, Pottsville Repulbican, Pottsville, PA, Jan 18, 1983.

46 Robert B Thompson death certificate, #0042512, #102079, Reg # 102, October 1907, Department of Vital records, New Castle, PA.

47 Robert B Thompson, Greenwood Cemetery, Tower City, Schuylkill Co, PA, John Barket, Tower City, PA, B-1-1.

48 Thompson family information, John L linden, jllinden@comcast.net.

49 Alexander Thompson, Schuylkill County, PA, p 1054.

50 Lydia B. Thompson, Greenwood Cemetery, Tower City, Schuylkill Co, PA, John Barket, Tower City, PA, B-1-1.

51 Robert B. Thompson, Greenwood Cemetery, Tower City, Schuylkill Co, PA, John Barket, Tower City, PA, B-3-1.

52 Thompson household, 1850 United States Census, Schuylkill Co, PA, ancestry.com & Microfilm, PA State Library, Hbg, PA.

53 Thompson household, 1860 United States Census, Schuylkill Co, PA, PA State library microfilm.

54 Thompson household, 1870 United States Census, Schuylkill Co, PA, ancestry.com & Microfilm, PA State Library, Hbg, PA.

55 Thompson household, 1880 United States Census, Dauphin Co, PA, FHL 1255124, Film T9-1124, p 432B, www.familysearch.org.

56 Pottsville Hospital, 1900 United States Census, Schuylkill Co, PA, T623, Roll 1485, p 189, www.ancestry.com and 1900 United States Census, Schuylkill Co, PA, PA State library microfilm image.

57 Thompson household, 1900 United States Census, Schuylkill Co, PA, T623, Roll 1485, p 189, www.ancestry.com and 1900 United States Census, Schuylkill Co, PA, PA State library microfilm image.

58 Robert B Thompson, Tower City, Valley Echo, October 20, 1883.

59 Lydia B. Thompson, Greenwood Cemetery, Tower City, Schuylkill Co, PA, John Barket, Tower City, PA, B-3-1.

60 Goodman household, 1870 United States Census, Dauphin Co, PA, ancestry.com & Microfilm, PA State Library, Hbg, PA.

61 Thompson family information, Irene C. Stearns, DeKalb, IL.

62 Bob Averell Family Tree, Bob Averell, raverell@carolina.rr.com, awt.ancestry.com.

63 Howard A.C. Hensel, #0036895, #63360, Reg # 66, June 1927, Department of Vital records, New Castle, PA.

64 Hensel family information, Victor Hensel, NJ.

65 Howard Andrew Carson Hensel, Howard Andrew Carson Hensel probate file, 1927, unnumbered orginal papers, 21pp, probated June 29, 1927, Schuylkill Co Courthouse, Schuylkill, PA, Norman Nicol, Apr 2008.

66 Clara M Hensel death certificate, #0042528, #37124, Reg # 29, March 1926, Department of Vital records, New Castle, PA.

67 Joseph Workman, Descendants of Joseph Workman, Evelyn S. Hartman.

68 Howard A.C. Hensel, Greenwood Cemetery, Tower City, Schuylkill Co, PA, John Barket, Tower City, PA, B-3-1.

69 Hentzel household, 1860 United States Census, Schuylkill Co, PA, ancestry.com & Microfilm, PA State Library, Hbg, PA.

70 Hentzel household, 1860 United States Census, Schuylkill Co, PA, PA State library microfilm.

71 Hensel household, 1870 United States Census, Dauphin Co, PA, PA State library microfilm.

72 Hensel household, 1880 United States Census, Dauphin Co, PA, FHL 1255124, Film T9-1124, p 270D, www.familysearch.org.

73 Hensel household, 1910 United States Census, Schuylkill Co, PA, www.ancestry.com and 1910 United States Census, Schuylkill Co, PA, ED 102, Sheet 4, PA State Library.

74 Hensel household, 1920 United States Census, Schuylkill Co, PA, T625 1652, p 17A, ED 143, Image 0877, www.ancestry.com and 1920 United States Census, Schuylkill Co, PA, PA State Libraray, microfilm image.

75 Hensel household, 1880 United States Census, Dauphin Co, PA, FHL 1255124, Film T9-1124, p 270D, www.familysearch.org.

76 Hensel household, 1920 United States Census, Schuylkill Co, PA, T625 1652, p 17A, ED 143, Image 0877, www.ancestry.com and 1920 United States Census, Schuylkill Co, PA, PA State Libraray, microfilm image.

77 Howard Andrew Carson Hensel, Washington Camp, Howard Andrew Carson Hensel probate file, 1927, unnumbered original papers, 21pp, probated June 29, 1927, Schuylkill Co Courthouse, Schuylkill, PA, Norman Nicol, Apr 2008.

78 Clara Hensel, Greenwood Cemetery, Tower City, Schuylkill Co, PA, John Barket, Tower City, PA, B-3-1.

79 Updegrove household, 1870 United States Census, Dauphin Co, PA, PA State library microfilm.

80 Updegrove household, 1880 United States Census, Dauphin Co, PA, www.ancestry.com and 1880 United States Census, Dauphin Co, PA, FHL 1255125, Film T9-1125, p 312B, www.familysearch.org.

81 Casper Hansel, Descendants of Casper (LaHentzelle) Hensel, Evelyn S Hartman, deanh@voicenet.com.

82 Thompson family information, Jim Thompson, jbthompson@compuserve.com, pp 4-11.

83 Thompson family information, Films from 1993, Jane L Fouraker, Lancaster Co, PA.

84 Thompson family information, Jim Thompson, jbthompson@compuserve.com, pp 4-11 & Thompson family information, Irene C. Stearns, DeKalb, IL.

85 Isabel Penman, Vital records Index, British Isles, Intellectual Reserve Inc, 8/5/2010.

86 Alexander Thompson, Schuylkill County, PA, p 668-669.

87 Alexander Thompson, Miners Journal, December 5, 1873.

88 Mrs.. Thompson, Burial record, Miners Journal deaths, 1851.

89 Alexander Thompson, Greenwood Cemetery, Tower City, Schuylkill Co, PA, John Barket, Tower City, PA, A-4-2.

90 Thompson household, 1840 United States Census, Schuylkill Co, PA, ancestry.com & Microfilm, PA State Library, Hbg, PA.

91 Thompson family information, Jennifer Bachman.

92 Thompson family information, James Thompson, jbthompson@compuserve.com.

93 Thompson family information, Signed November 1, 1836, Jim Thompson, jbthompson@compuserve.com, pp 4-11.

94 Alexander Thompson, November 1836, Court of Common Pleas, Schuylkill Co, PA.

95 Alexander Thompson, Dauphin Co Biograhpical Encyclopedia.

96 Tower City Centennial.

97 Alexander Thompson, Reg of Wills, Bk 4, pp 142-3; probate file, 1873, unnumbered original papers, 10pp, Schuylkill Co Courthouse, Schuylkill, PA, Norman Nicol, Apr 2008.

98 Alexander Thompson, Sheridan, Pottsville & Schuylkill Co, PA, J.H. Zerbey, pp 1131-1132.

99 Mrs.. Thompson, Burial record, Miners Journal deaths, April 1851.

100 Penman family information, Jim Thompson, jbthompson@compuserve.com.

101 Michael Goodman, Tower City, Porter Centennial, 1868-1968, p 188.

102 Michael Goodman, Obituatary, FROM 'THE WEST SCHUYLKILL HERALD', 03 JANUARY 1901, Jeffrey A. Brown, ntrprz@dmv.com.

103 Michael Gurtmann, "Pennsylvania, Births and Christenings, 1709-1950," index, FamilySearch (https://familysearch.org/pal:/MM9.1.1/V2NX-KXS : accessed 19 Nov 2014), Michael Gutmann, 12 May 1811; Christening, citing SAINT JOHNS LUTHERAN CHURCH NEAR BERRYSBURG,MIFFLIN TWP,DAUPHIN,PENNSYLVANIA; FHL microfilm 845111.

104 Michael Goodman death certificate, #1252, May 1901, Dauphin County Register of Wills, Harrisburg, PA.

105 Goodman household, 1840 United States Census, Schuylkill Co, PA, Roll M704 492, p 79, Image 159, ancestry.com & Microfilm, PA State Library, Hbg, PA.

106 Goodman household, 1850 United States Census, Dauphin Co, PA, 338, ancestry.com & Microfilm, PA State Library, Hbg, PA.

107 Goodman household, 1860 United States Census, Dauphin Co, PA, ancestry.com & Microfilm, PA State Library, Hbg, PA.

108 Goodman household, 1880 United States Census, Dauphin Co, PA, www.ancestry.com and 1880 United States Census, Dauphin Co, PA, FHL 1255124, Film T9-1124, p 432B, www.familysearch.org.

109 Goodman household, 1900 United States Census, Dauphin Co, PA, www.ancestry.com and 1900 United States Census, Dauphin Co, PA, Pa State Library microfilm image.

110 Michael Gutman, St. Peter's Evangelical Lutheran Church, Reinertown, PA, Pastor Arthur Sonnenberg, July 6, 2005.

111 Goodman household, 1850 United States Census, Dauphin Co, PA, 338, ancestry.com & Microfilm, PA State Library, Hbg, PA.

112 Goodman household, 1860 United States Census, Dauphin Co, PA, ancestry.com & Microfilm, PA State Library, Hbg, PA.

113 Goodman household, 1880 United States Census, Dauphin Co, PA, www.ancestry.com and 1880 United States Census, Dauphin Co, PA, FHL 1255124, Film T9-1124, p 432B, www.familysearch.org.

114 Michael Goodman, Probate files, 1901, Inventory, 3-173, Aff. of Death, Bk D, p434, Dauphin County Courthouse, Reg of Wills, Deborah Hershey, Elizabethtown, PA, Mar 2008.

115 Brown household, 1820 United States Census, Schuylkill Co, PA, ancestry.com & Microfilm, PA State Library, Hbg, PA.

116 Brown household, 1830 United States Census, Dauphin Co, PA, ancestry.com & Microfilm, PA State Library, Hbg, PA.

117 Goodman household, 1870 United States Census, Dauphin Co, PA, ancestry.com & Microfilm, PA State Library, Hbg, PA.

118 Hensel-Workman marriage record, 1853, Register of Wills, Dauphin Co, PA.

119 Hensel family information, Dauphin Co Marriages, 1852-1855, CAGS.

120 Hensel family information, History of Michael Hensel (Hentzel) Sr. & His Related Families, R. Longtin-Thompson.

121 Andrew Gise Hensel death certificate, #0036891, #115081, Reg # 84, December 1908, Department of Vital records, New Castle, PA.

122 Andrew Gise Hensel, #0036891, #115081, Reg # 84, December 1908, Department of Vital records, New Castle, PA.

123 Hensel household, 1840 United States Census, Perry Co, PA, ancestry.com & Microfilm, PA State Library, Hbg, PA.

124 Hensil household, 1850 United States Census, Perry Co, PA, Roll M432-805, p 433, Image 283, ancestry.com & Microfilm, PA State Library, Hbg, PA.

125 Hentzel household, 1860 United States Census, Schuylkill Co, PA, M653-1181, 628-9, ancestry.com & Microfilm, PA State Library, Hbg, PA.

126 Hensel household, 1870 United States Census, Dauphin Co, PA, M593-1335, 997-566, ancestry.com & Microfilm, PA State Library, Hbg, PA.

127 Hensel household, 1880 United States Census, Dauphin Co, PA, FHL 1255124, Film T9-1124, p 270D, 71-76, www.familysearch.org.

128 Weist household, 1900 United States Census, Dauphin Co, PA, Roll T623 1404, p 2A, ED 190, ancestry.com & Microfilm, PA State Library, Hbg, PA.

129 Andrew Henzel, Anton Hentschel, Civil war Soldier & Sailor System, M554, Roll 53, http://www.itd.nps.gov/cwss/soldiers.cfm.

130 Andrew Henzel, US Civil War Soldiers, 1861-1865, M554 roll 53, www.ancestry.com.

131 Andrew Hensel, Andrew Hensel, Private, 47th Reg, Co F, NY Inf [Civil War to 1900 Pension index, footnote.com.

132 Andrew Henson, Andrew Henson [Union Inf, 107th Reg, PA. from Hbg, Civil War Soldiers & Sailors, www.itd.nps.gov/cwss/].

133 Hentzel household, 1860 United States Census, Schuylkill Co, PA, PA State library microfilm.

134 Hensel household, 1870 United States Census, Dauphin Co, PA, PA State library microfilm.

135 Weist household, 1900 United States Census, Dauphin Co, PA, Roll T623 1404, p 2A, ED 190, ancestry.com & Microfilm, PA State Library, Hbg, PA.

136 Heheel household, 1900 United States Census, Dauphin Co, PA, Roll T623 1404, p 2A, ED 190, ancestry.com & Microfilm, PA State Library, Hbg, PA.

137 Workman household, 1840 United States Census, Dauphin Co, PA, ancestry.com & Microfilm, PA State Library, Hbg, PA.

138 Workman household, 1850 United States Census, Dauphin Co, PA, PA State library microfilm.

139 Daniel Updegrove death certificate, #1071, March 1899, Dauphin County Register of Wills, Harrisburg, PA.

140 Updegrove Family information, Updegrove Genealogy, PA State library.

141 Daniel Updegrove, Vital records, Dauphin County, p 26.

142 Mrs. Sarah Updegrove death certificate, #0042525, #81494, File 42, Reg 2193, July 1923, Department of Vital Records, New Castle, PA.

143 Daniel Updegrove, Vital records, Dauphin County, p 26.

144 Bastoe household, 1850 United States Census, Dauphin Co, PA ancestry.com & Microfilm, PA State Library, Hbg, PA.

145 Updegrove household, 1850 United States Census, Dauphin Co, PA, PA State library microfilm.

146 Hullsizer household, 1860 United States Census, Lycoming Co, PA, ancestry.com & Microfilm, PA State Library, Hbg, PA.

147 Updegrove household, 1870 United States Census, Dauphin Co, PA, Roll 1335, p 792, Jan.

148 Updegrove household, 1850 United States Census, Dauphin Co, PA ancestry.com & Microfilm, PA State Library, Hbg, PA.

149 Daniel Updegrove, Schuylkill Countians captured in the Civil War, rootsweb.com.

150 Daniel Updegrove, Civil War Pension Index, www.ancestry.com.

151 Daniel Updegrove, Schuylkill Countians captured in the Civil War, rootsweb.com.

152 Daniel Updegrave, 1864-5 service, 1890 Veterans Schedule, private, Tower City, Schuylkill Co, PA, Roll 83, p 3, ED 215, www.ancestry.com.

153 Daniel Updegrove, Civil War Pension Index, K 39 PA infantry, filed 1899, www.ancestry.com.

154 Daniel Updegrove, Daniel Updegrave, Co B, 9 Reg, PA Cav, App #7-05327 Cert #737767 & App #530812, Cert #326251, footnote.com.

155 Daniel Updegrove, Civil War Veterans Card File, 1861-1866, PA State Archives, www.digitalarchives.state.pa.us.

156 Culp household, 1850 United States Census, Union Co, PA, ancestry.com & Microfilm, PA State Library, Hbg, PA.

157 Culp household, 1860 United States Census, Union Co, PA, ancestry.com & Microfilm, PA State Library, Hbg, PA.

158 Updegrove household, 1900 United States Census, Juniata, PA, ancestry.com & Microfilm, PA State Library, Hbg, PA.

159 Shadel household, 1910 United States Census, Dauphin Co, PA, ED 0133, Visit 0014, www.ancestry.com and 1910 United States Census, Dauphin Co, PA, ED 133, Sheet 1, PA State Library microfilm image.

160 Weist household, 1920 United States Census, Schuylkill Co, PA, ED 143, sheet A, PA State Library, microfilm image.

161 Culp household, 1850 United States Census, Union Co, PA, ancestry.com & Microfilm, PA State Library, Hbg, PA.

162 Sarah Salome Updegrove, Probate files, Roll 43, U4, Dauphin County Courthouse, Reg of Wills, Harrisburg, PA, Deborah Hershey, Elizabethtown, PA, Mar 2008.

163 Daniel Updegrove, Civil War Pension Index: General Index to Pension Files, 1861-1934, www.ancestry.com.

164 Robert Thompson, Ancestry Publci trees, O'Brien Family Tree, Owner: christine hillstead, ancestry.com.

165 Thompson family information, Jane Fouraker, mjfour@mindpsring.com.

166 Robert Thompson, Thompson History, Jim Thompson, jbthompson@compuserve.com, pp 4-11, Thompson family information, John B. Linden, Lynden@comcast.net.

167 David Penman, FHL, Pedigree chart, www.ancestry.com.

168 David Penman, Penman family information, John Penman, PenmanJC@aol.com.

169 Penman family information, John Penman, JCPenman@aol.com.

170 Pennman household, 1840 United States Census, Schuylkill Co, PA, ancestry.com & Microfilm, PA State Library, Hbg, PA.

171 Elizabeth Penman, 1841 Scotland Census Record, Midlothian, SCO, www.ancestry.com.

172 John Penman, Vital records Index, British Isles, Intellectual Reserve Inc, 8/5/2010.

173 Goodman family data, DESCENDANTS OF GEORGE GOODMAN OF BETHEL TOWNSHIP, BERKS CO, Lawrence Goodman, lawrenceeg@comcast.net, http://www.goodmangenealogy.com/1104.htm.

174 Michael Gudman, Bethel. January 25, 1810., http://berks.pa-roots.com/.

175 Peter Brown, Tyson Family_2012-03-18 , Owner: Gary Tyson, ancestry.com.

176 Brown family information, Peter Brown descedants, Deb Kandybowksi, debkandy@epix.net.

177 Brown household, 1790 United States Census, Berks Co, PA, ancestry.com & Microfilm, PA State Library, Hbg, PA.

178 Brown household, 1820 United States Census, York Co, PA, ancestry.com.

179 Brown household, 1810 United States Census, Berks Co, PA ancestry.com & Microfilm, PA State Library, Hbg, PA.

180 Brown household, 1820 United States Census, Dauphin Co, PA, ancestry.com & Microfilm, PA State Library, Hbg, PA.

181 Brown household, 1830 United States Census, Dauphin Co, PA ancestry.com & Microfilm, PA State Library, Hbg, PA.

182 Brown household, 1840 United States Census, Dauphin Co, PA ancestry.com & Microfilm, PA State Library, Hbg, PA.

183 Brown household, 1850 United States Census, Dauphin Co, PA, p 336, Kathleen M Fagnani, katfagn@erols.com.

184 Brown household, 1850 United States Census, Dauphin Co, PA, 338, ancestry.com & Microfilm, PA State Library, Hbg, PA.

185 Peter Braun, Schuylkill County, PA, Chicago, JH Beers & Co, 1916, vol II, p 1071, Historical Society of Schuylkill County.

186 Maria Brown, McCallister's Methodist Cemetery, Barbara, Homelybin@aol.com.

187 Brown household, 1860 United States Census, Dauphin Co, PA, ancestry.com & Microfilm, PA State Library, Hbg, PA.

188 Andreas Hansel, Baptism, York Co, PA library, cards on file.

189 Andrew Hensel, Christ Church, Littlestown, PA, Adams Co County 18th records lookup, Virginia, vperry1@shawneelink.net.

190 Andrew Hensel, Death of an Old Soldier, Obituary, New Bloomfield newspaper, July 1875.

191 Andrew Hensel, Source 146, index card, Perry County Historians.

192 Mrs. Hensel, Source 140 & 146, index cards, Perry County Historians.

193 Mrs. Mary Hensel, New Bloomfield Times, January 20, 1877.

194 Mary Hensel, U.S., Find A Grave Index, 1600s, Ancestry.com. U.S., Find A Grave Index, 1600s-Current [database on-line]. Provo, UT, USA: Ancestry.com Operations, Inc., 2012. Original data: Find A Grave. Find A Grave. http://www.findagrave.com/cgi-bin/fg.cgi.

195 Andrew Hensel, Union Lutheran Cemetery, New Bloomfield, Perry Co, PA, 30 Perry Co PA Cemetery Records, Closson Press, Apollo, PA, 1992.

196 Hensel household, 1800 United States Census, York Co, PA, ancestry.com & Microfilm, PA State Library, Hbg, PA.

197 Hinsle household, 1820 United States Census, Adams Co, PA, ancestry.com & Microfilm, PA State Library, Hbg, PA.

198 Henzell household, 1830 United States Census, Perry Co, PA, ancestry.com & Microfilm, PA State Library, Hbg, PA.

199 Hensley household, 1840 United States Census, Perry Co, PA, ancestry.com & Microfilm, PA State Library, Hbg, PA.

200 Miller household, 1860 United States Census, Perry Co, PA, PA State library microfilm.

201 Hentzelle household, 1870 United States Census, Perry Co, PA, PA State library microfilm.

202 Andrew Hensel, War of 1812 Records, DDC, 1999-, www.ancestry.com.

203 Churches Between the Mountains, A History of the Lutheran Congregatioons in Perry County, PA,. D.H. Focht.

204 Andrew Hensel, Probate files, 1875, rep 49, Perry County Historicans, Newport, PA, Deborah Hershey, Elizabethtown, PA, Jan 2009.

205 Andrew Hensel, 1878, August 02, 1875, Dauphin County Register of Wills, Harrisburg, PA.

206 Andrew Hentzell, Adams Co Centinel, Gettysburg, PA, October 8, 1823.

207 Andrew Hensel, Andrew Hensel, Death of an Old Soldier, Obituary, New Bloomfield newspaper, July 1875.

208 Mary Hensel, Union Lutheran Cemetery, New Bloomfield, Perry Co, PA, 30 Perry Co PA Cemetery Records, Closson Press, Apollo, PA, 1992.

209 Guise household, 1800 United States Census, Adams Co, PA, ancestry.com & Microfilm, PA State Library, Hbg, PA.

210 Guise household, 1810 United States Census, Adams Co, PA, ancestry.com & Microfilm, PA State Library, Hbg, PA.

211 Guise household, 1820 United States Census, Adams Co, PA, ancestry.com & Microfilm, PA State Library, Hbg, PA.

212 Workman family information, Evelyn Hartman, Evelyn S Hartman, deanh@voicenet.com.

213 Joseph Workman, Wiconisco Calvary Cemetery, Rhonda, yeahbaby@penn.com, Row 4.

214 Joseph Workman, U.S., Find A Grave Index, 1600s, Ancestry.com. U.S., Find A Grave Index, 1600s-Current [database on-line]. Provo, UT, USA: Ancestry.com Operations, Inc., 2012. Original data: Find A Grave. Find A Grave. http://www.findagrave.com/cgi-bin/fg.cgi.

215 .

.

216 The Romberger Line, Ancestors of Richard Alan Lebo.

217 Romberger Family, St. John's Lutheran Church, p 10, John Romberger.

218 Workman household, 1820 United States Census, Dauphin Co, PA, ancestry.com & Microfilm, PA State Library, Hbg, PA.

219 Workman household, 1830 United States Census, Dauphin Co, PA, ancestry.com & Microfilm, PA State Library, Hbg, PA.

220 Workman household, 1850 United States Census, Union Co, PA, FTM CD 305, Disk 4, film 775.

221 Joseph Workman Sr, Probate files, 1857, Letter of Admin, A-35, Dauphin County Courthouse, Reg of Wills, Deborah Hershey, Elizabethtown, PA, Mar 2008.

222 Workman, PA Births, Dauphin County, J. Humphrey.

223 Susan Romberger, Baptism Balthaser & Elizabeth, St. Johns (Hill) Church, Lykens, Dauphin Co, PA, PA Births, Dauphin County, J. Humphrey.

224 Romberger household, 1800 United States Census, Dauphin Co, PA, ancestry.com & Microfilm, PA State Library, Hbg, PA.

225 Romberger household, 1810 United States Census, Dauphin Co, PA, ancestry.com & Microfilm, PA State Library, Hbg, PA.

226 Johann Uptegrav, 1805, Jacobs Church, Pine Grove, Swedberg, SCUR III, p 240.

227 Updegrove Family information, Rosie Byard, rbyard@bigfoot.com.

228 John Upderove, Smith Family Tree, Owner: hannibal8901, ancestry.com.

229 Rutzel Family Genealogy, David Rutzel, leztur@hotmail.com, awt.ancestry.com.

230 Elizabeth Reiss, Provizzi Family Tree, Owner: sprovizzi, ancestry.com.

231 Updegrove household, 1810 United States Census, Dauphin Co, PA, ancestry.com & Microfilm, PA State Library, Hbg, PA.

232 Updegrove household, 1820 United States Census, Dauphin Co, PA, ancestry.com & Microfilm, PA State Library, Hbg, PA.

233 Updagrove household, 1830 United States Census, Berks Co, PA, ancestry.com & Microfilm, PA State Library, Hbg, PA.

234 Updegraf household, 1840 United States Census, Dauphin Co, PA, ancestry.com & Microfilm, PA State Library, Hbg, PA.

235 Updegrove household, 1860 United States Census, Lycoming Co, PA, ancestry.com & Microfilm, PA State Library, Hbg, PA.

236 Kulp family information, J. Wagner, Union County.

237 Mrs Elizabeth Kulp, Pennsylvania and New Jersey, Church and Town Records, 1708-1985 about Mrs Elizabeth Culp. Source Citation: Historical Society of Pennsylvania; Historic Pennsylvania Church and Town Records; Reel: 234.

238 Culp household, 1850 United States Census, Union Co, PA, FTM CD 305, Disk 10, film 831.

239 Culp household, 1860 United States Census, Union Co, PA, ancestry.com & Microfilm, PA State Library, Hbg, PA.

240 Elizabeth Culp, findagrave.com.

241 Schneck household, 1810 United States Census, Northumberland Co, PA, ancestry.com & Microfilm, PA State Library, Hbg, PA.

242 Schneck household, 1820 United States Census, Union Co, PA, ancestry.com & Microfilm, PA State Library, Hbg, PA.

NARRATIVE SOURCES

1 http://civilwar.gratzpa.org/2012/01/alexander-f-thompson-senator-and-attorney/

2 http://coalregionhistorychronicles.blogspot.com/2008/09/explosion-at-york-farm-colliery.html

3 http://www.dailykos.com/story/2013/09/22/1211516/-Sweet-Home-Schuylkill-County-The-PA-Anthracite-coal-region-1790-1917#

4 http://en.wikipedia.org/wiki/Ludlow_Massacre

5 http://civilwar.gratzpa.org/2012/01/alexander-f-thompson-senator-and-attorney/

6 http://ultimatehistoryproject.com/before-the-whiteout-wedding-dresses-and-grooms-outfits.html

7 http://coalregionhistorychronicles.blogspot.com/2008/09/explosion-at-york-farm-colliery.html

8 http://usminedisasters.com/Mine_Disasters/search_Coal_state.asp?ACC_STATE_NAME=Pennsylvania&x=11&y=15

9 Schuylkill County Firefighting by Michael R. Glore and Michael J. Kitsock. Arcadia Publishing, 2010.

10 http://civilwar.gratzpa.org/veterans/

11 Charles McKean, "Edinburgh: 3. 1750 Onwards" in: The Oxford Companion to Scottish History, Edited by Michael Lynch, OUP, 2007.

12 http://civilwar.gratzpa.org/2012/01/alexander-f-thompson-senator-and-attorney/; http://www.findagrave.com/cgi-bin/fg.cgi?page=gr&GRid=117381891

13 http://civilwar.gratzpa.org/2012/01/alexander-f-thompson-senator-and-attorney/

14 http://www.findagrave.com/cgi-bin/fg.cgi?page=gr&GRid=62785330

15 http://civilwar.gratzpa.org/2012/01/alexander-f-thompson-senator-and-attorney/

16 http://www.measuringworth.com/uscompare/relativevalue.php

17 http://files.usgwarchives.net/pa/schuylkill/history/local/munsell/hist0012.txt

18 https://books.google.com/books?id=eCk_AQAAMAAJ&pg=PA159&lpg=PA159&dq=Bast+%26+Thompson+Schuylkill+county+mines&source=bl&ots=CWTape7T1m&sig=Qm3SW59QO91reKpIleicM0cI0UU&hl=en&sa=X&ei=9Jj-VPrtCMu0ggTCrYHgDA&ved=0CC4Q6AEwAw#v=onepage&q=Bast%20%26%20Thompson%20Schuylkill%20county%20mines&f=false

19 http://explorepahistory.com/story.php?storyId=1-9-4

20 http://www.measuringworth.com/uscompare

21 http://explorepahistory.com/story.php?storyId=1-9-4

22 http://www.digitalarchives.state.pa.us/archive.asp?view=ArchiveItems&ArchiveID=17&FL=G&FID=1194432&LID=1194481

23 Tower City, Porter Township Centennial book, 1868-1968, Records of Jim Thompson, jbthompson@compuserve.com]

24 FROM 'THE WEST SCHUYLKILL HERALD', 03 JANUARY 1901, Jeffrey A. Brown, ntrprz@dmv.com]

25 https://www.lycoming.edu/umarch/chronicles/2011/2Evangelical.pdf

26 http://www.ebooksread.com/authors-eng/jm-runk--company/commemorative-biographical-encyclopedia-of-dauphin-county-pennsylvania--contai-urm/page-198-commemorative-biographical-encyclopedia-of-dauphin-county-pennsylvania--cont ai-urm.shtml

27 https://books.google.com/books?id=rRwQAAAAYAAJ&pg=PA308&lpg=PA308&dq=Captain+John+McMillan%E2%80%99s+company,+Colonel+Fenton%E2%80%99s+regiment,+of+the+Pennsylvania+Militia&source=bl&ots=YpSCK5C7sj&sig=hKIwaYSwScmid-HNUo_kavB2_EE&hl=en&sa=X&ei=_cpfVfnLMczBsAXt-YAI&ved=0CDIQ6AEwBA#v=onepage&q=Captain%20John%20McMillan%E2%80%99s%20company%2C%20Colonel%20Fenton%E2%80%99s%20regiment%2C%20of%20the%20Pennsylvania%20Militia&f=false

28 https://archive.org/stream/troopsundercomma01harr/troopsundercomma01harr_djvu.txt

29 http://www.dailykos.com/story/2013/09/23/1211516/-Sweet-Home-Schuylkill-County-The-PA-Anthracite-coal-region-1790-1917.

30 http://historynewsnetwork.org/article/623.

31 History of Pennsylvania volunteers, 1861-5; prepared in compliance with acts of the legislature, by Samuel P. Bates. Collection: Making of America Books http://quod.lib.umich.edu/m/moa/aby3439.0004.001/818?page=root;sid=41cea510eb7635c5b3e50413737b17fb;size=100;view=image;q1=One+Hundred+And+Fifty-Fifth+Regiment

32 History of Pennsylvania volunteers, 1861-5; prepared in compliance with acts of the legislature, by Samuel P. Bates. Collection: Making of America Books http://quod.lib.umich.edu/m/moa/aby3439.0004.001/818?page=root;sid=41cea510eb7635c5b3e50413737b17fb;size=100;view=image;q1=One+Hundred+And+Fifty-Fifth+Regiment.

33 Under the Maltese Cross (1910), available at https://books.google.com/books?id=zag-AAAAYAAJ&printsec=frontcover&source=gbs_ge_summary_r&cad=0#v=onepage&q=hensel&f=false; After the Reserves: An Unofficial History of the 190th and 191st Pennsylvania Volunteer Infantry Regiments, June 1, 1864 through June 28, 1865, available at

http://www.pareserves.com/files/pdf_files/AFTER%20THE%20RESERVES.PDF

34 http://zouavedatabase.weebly.com/civil-war-zouave-unit-master-list.html

35 http://155thpa.tripod.com/id2.html - see pictures of the uniforms here.

36 Title: History of Pennsylvania volunteers, 1861-5; prepared in compliance with acts of the legislature, by Samuel P. Bates.

37 Author: Bates, Samuel P. (Samuel Penniman), 1827-1902.

38 Collection: Making of America Books
http://quod.lib.umich.edu/m/moa/aby3439.0004.001/818?page=root;sid=41cea510e
b7635c5b3e50413737b17fb;size=100;view=image;q1=One+Hundred+And+Fifty-F
ifth+Regiment

39 http://www.pacivilwar.com/regiment/155th.html and
http://www.pacivilwar.com/regiment/191st.html

40 http://civilwar.gratzpa.org/2012/04/2012-additions-to-civil-war-veterans-list-g-
to-i/

41
http://civilwar.gratzpa.org/2011/01/tower-city-porter-township-centennial-civil-war
-veterans-list/

42 http://www.civilwararchive.com/Unreghst/unpacav1.htm#9th

43 http://www.lancasteratwar.com/2011/12/here-comes-cavalry-part-ii-lochiel.html

44 "A Scout to East Tennessee by the Lochiel Cavalry." Anecdotes, Poetry, and Incidents of the War: North and South : 1860-1865, By Frank Moore
https://books.google.com/books?id=xr-rrOqOPysC&pg=PA553&lpg=PA553&dq=
Lochiel+Cavalry+and+libby+prison&source=bl&ots=31SzP5eI6A&sig=g46Cqj-M
4kAZOwYpx5fCh84j6Oo&hl=en&sa=X&ved=0CEMQ6AEwBmoVChMIgr6vufq
nxwIVw4MNCh0nyA2A#v=onepage&q=Lochiel%20&f=false

45 Luther Reily Kelker, History of Dauphin County, Pennsylvania: With Genealogical Memoirs, Volumes 1-2, p. 1080

46
https://books.google.com/books?id=j3NWAAAAYAAJ&pg=PA1080&lpg=PA108
0&dq=solomon+updegrove+d.+1864+georgia&source=bl&ots=8iZFQh28Zi&sig=
XR_F0FkDZ9F8_9Bp206AZktxp2I&hl=en&sa=X&ved=0CB8Q6AEwAGoVChM
IhbGV5_G7xwIVDOCACh138gBg#v=onepage&q=solomon%20updegrove%20d.
%201864%20georgia&f=false;
http://www.findagrave.com/cgi-bin/fg.cgi?page=gr&GRid=84377395

47 http://files.usgwarchives.net/pa/schuylkill/military/civilwar/captured.txt

48 https://en.wikipedia.org/wiki/Libby_Prison_Escape

49
http://www.civilwar.org/education/history/warfare-and-logistics/warfare/richmond.

html

50 http://www.rootsweb.ancestry.com/~padauph2/lykinsnews.html

51 http://www.rootsweb.ancestry.com/~padauph2/lykinsnews.html

52 Weekly Notes of Cases Argued and Determined in the Supreme Court ...,
Volume 20
https://books.google.com/books?id=MT-TAAAAIAAJ&pg=PA179&dq=%22danie
l+updegrove%22&hl=en&sa=X&ved=0CC4Q6AEwA2oVChMI_67k2MKnxwIVy
6CACh1IaQDu#v=onepage&q=daniel%20updegrove&f=false

53 http://www.pagenweb.org/~schuylkill/castle/castle19.jpg

ABOUT THE AUTHORS

Marc D. Thompson delved into writing and genealogy at a very early age. He wrote stories, poems, lyrics and family history books. Marc went on to write and research in high school and college, earning a BS degree from Moravian College. He has presented genealogical lectures and authored over thirteen family history volumes. Marc's other published works include The Fitness Book of Lists, Virtual Personal Training Manual, Fitness Quotes of Humorous Inspiration and a poetry compilation, He currently pens a genealogy blog at google blogger and wrote a monthly genealogy column for Atlantic Avenue Magazine. He is a member of the Association of Professional Genealogists, founded a PA Genealogy Society and was the County Coordinator of the Chatham Co, GA USGenweb site. Marc believes in what he calls Creatalytical Thinking: The fusion of creativity and analysis to view life more fully and fulfill his place in this world. Writing now for over four decades, Marc has been influenced by science, art and his relationships, and yet marvels at the cosmically-driven direction he receives from energy around him.

Tom Sullivan, after returning from service in Mongolia with the US Peace Corps in 2010, started working as a freelancer, providing writing and editorial services in fields related to his previous work experiences as a teacher, writer and editor. Tom is skilled in academic, educational, instructional, technical, marketing, sales, and journalistic writing styles. He also enjoys and is comfortable working with non-native speakers/writers of English. In addition to freelancing, Tom teaches composition courses at Blue River Community College in Independence, Missouri. Tom enjoys the variety and challenge of his work and spends his free time on artistic pursuits such as cooking and writing. Tom is a member of the Editorial Freelancers Association.

INDEX OF INDIVIDUALS

INDEX OF INDIVIDUALS

INDEX OF INDIVIDUALS

www.ingramcontent.com/pod-product-compliance
Lightning Source LLC
Chambersburg PA
CBHW081156270326
41930CB00014B/3172